CAIN, WHERE IS YOUR BROTHER?

Cain,
Where Is Your Brother?

by

FRANÇOIS MAURIAC

COWARD-McCANN, INC.
NEW YORK

Contents

CONTENTS

Preface

SONS, friends—the sweetest names of the human language, which express the best and purest that has been given us in this world—behold the stakes of the criminal game to which we are being dragged by madmen whom we did not know how to strangle when there was still time.

After a respite of fifteen years, we are once more on the verge of war—undoubtedly the worst and most bitter in the history of men. Perhaps for the last time, our turn has come again to drink this chalice which peoples have been passing from hand to hand since the time men first came upon the earth and began slaughtering one another.

Our leaders appear to have done all that is humanly possible to push this bitter cup far from us, and no people of any epoch was ever more unwillingly forced than ours to bring it to its lips. But, even if just, war is evil and therefore not of God. What is of God is this force in us which submits to the horrible event as we would to a master that He gives us by His own hand. Let us then receive "these sacraments of the present moment" of which Père de Caussade speaks, terrifying as they may be in appearance. Bodies will be crushed, spirits humiliated by the abominable unreason that is about to reign on earth. But the order of charity remains—the inner kingdom that is not of this world and whose peace is not at the mercy of any *Führer*, of any wild man.

The reflections that follow represent my partial, incomplete effort to illuminate the inner kingdom with regard to particular people, events, or circumstances that define my own life's drama. I cannot testify that there is spiritual nutriment in them for everyone, or even for anyone but myself, but if in the evening of his life, any old man ever wished to gather up the fragments of peace, lest they be lost, I am he!

F. M.

CAIN, WHERE IS YOUR BROTHER?

Our Leaders and Their Critics

THERE is always an hour of the night when the master of a great number of men finds himself alone with himself between four walls. There, burrowed in the secrecy of his lair, the panting wolf licks his wounds. Then he discovers that during this interminable day, while he was being harassed by petitioners and delegates, while he was presiding at ceremonies and arbitrating conflicts, he had not stopped losing blood and that unwittingly he has already completed more than half of the journey toward that other shore from which our loved ones call us, and where the arrows of the hunters no longer reach us.

The more public one's life, the more a man needs a hidden tenderness; the more we are exposed to public gaze and attack, the more we need the shadow of a sheltering heart. I do not know what a political man is, but I know what a single writer is: invulnerable in the company of those whom he loves and who cherish him, but so easily attacked the moment that he once more finds himself alone!

Undoubtedly the pen would fall from the hands of pitiless critics were they able to see the silent film unroll in the life of a public man. The latter's prominence may surpass imagination while the sun is shining, but when evening unfolds, he is the most forsaken of men in the great city. He looks, in the middle of the night, on the tile floor of a small kitchen, for the place where, eighteen months before, his wife had perhaps lain down to die. His enemies could not even imagine this scene . . . but his friends?

It is not natural for a man to feel pity for such masters: he hates them or he adores them, he venerates or despises them. But he has no pity for them.

A public servant of this type evokes the concept of power. The idea that it may be a duty to deal gently, as one would with a weak adversary, with the man who rules over towns, over all the police forces of the State or the National Guard could never occur to a controversialist who, believing he is aiming at Goliath, knows himself to be cruel perhaps, but thinks himself to be standing in the footsteps of David.

Pascal says that it would be necessary to have a highly filtered mind to regard the great lord surrounded by forty thousand Janissaries in his seraglio as just an average man. A journalist or critic of the opposition would have to have an even more filtered mind to divine that this public servant who has both Congress and the populace on his side is in reality a creature pressed to the point of his final resistance—a poor helpless quarry.

What man would imagine that a general of the army or a president of his country could be this man who, in the evening of an exhausting day, finds himself alone in a small apartment—this forsaken man whose housekeeper has not even waited for him, and whose supper is growing cold on a corner of the table between two plates?

Of whatever party we are members, it is up to us to create an impassioned atmosphere, which calumny cannot traverse, around the leaders whom we love. Love, not laws, protects them against defamation. No press bill will prevent the born controversialist from barking at the heels of the powerful whom he hates, and collecting anything and everything which can be damaging to them, which can destroy them. Will it help at all, after the poor man has been driven to suicide by despair, for the masses to be set in motion to honor his memory?

Much more than the approbation of a million partisans around his funeral bier would have been the presence of a single friend at the hour when others go away, when he was alone and stripped of all the deceits and trappings of august power that cease to exist when they are outside human observation.

A Certain Look

SUMMER in this country of Valois is only the confused coming together of spring and autumn. The last cherries that we eat are wet with a mist which in the morning already gives off the smell of harvested crops. Even in the sun, I cannot stretch myself out on the meadows without being seized by the cold of the clay.

I know that summer reigns elsewhere and that its kingdom mingles with that of my childhood: *It's 95° in the shade*, someone writes to me from Malagar. *We have had no rain for three months. Everything is scorched: there will be no early harvests, apart from some potatoes. Water is lacking: we are going to look for it at Garonne for the sulphating and for sprinkling the cypresses. But the vine is not suffering.* In other times I was like the vine: this murderous season overexcited me, I defied the fire of heaven: "We don't even take the livestock out, and here you run along the roads?" people said to me. Yes, I ran along the roads, I sang in the fiery furnace like the three youths of the Bible.

It pleases me to know that the furnace still exists, but I am also glad to be liberated from it. Parched landscapes no longer attract me. I have established my dwelling, between spring and autumn, in this Valois that has only three seasons. The spirit rejoices in its own awakening under the shade of these foliages, saturated with water, and in this turbid sun.

At this turning at which I have arrived, how distant seem those orgies of reading in which I indulged during the vacations of other times, when they said: "This child devours everything . . . we don't know what else to give him!" Today only a few lines suffice which I ruminate and whose quintessence I never exhaust. In the old house full of books I go from Montaigne to La Bruyère, from Cardinal de Retz to Saint-Simon, but sometimes it is a modern who gives me the joy of touching the truth, of holding it captive and alive in a few simple and irreplaceable words. For example, these days I am reading to myself what Chesterton wrote about St. Francis of Assisi:

> St. Francis deliberately did not see the wood for the trees. It is even more true that he deliberately did not see the mob for the men. . . . He only saw the image of God multiplied but never monotonous. To him a man was always a man and did not disappear in a dense crowd any more than in a desert. He honored all men . . . he not only loved but respected them all. . . . There was never a man who looked into those brown burning eyes without being certain that Francis Bernardone was really interested in *him*, in his own inner individual life from the cradle to the grave, that he himself was being valued and taken seriously. . . .

Chesterton's words describe a spiritual homeland in which all of us, of the left and right, should one day meet. Or at least all of us who, as a companion of Gide in his journey to the USSR wrote, cannot accustom ourselves to the imbecilic relations that one has with human beings from one end of the world to the other.

It is not only our ideas that separate us, that make us fight with one another day by day, hour by hour. But there is a certain personal stance we take within ourselves, a certain quality in the look that we fix on others. There is, for instance, André Gide's "look" at the USSR, which he admired to the point of a sickening obsession, and there is Georges Bernanos' intensely vital view of Majorca. These two writers, so different from each other, have this in common: a clear eye which can penetrate, can even at times disclose, the law of the human jungle.

Not the look of Jean-Jacques Rousseau, to be sure, who was incapable of grasping that nature is wounded. The knowledge and the love of man, such as he is, should not blind us to his misery, to his ferocity, or win us over to institutions that accord him too much trust. True love can only make us hostile to every doctrine that diverts him from his soul, from this kingdom within himself.

It looks like a very simple thing to see a man where there is a man, and not a camel, a horse or a spider. It is nevertheless this clear eye, this absence of madness, which today pass for madness—above all where such humbug as "creativity," "drive" and "singularity" are pushed to the point where the life of the creature has an absolute value. Nothing makes us more insufferable to everybody,

friends and foes alike, then to call an assassin an assassin, and an innocent man innocent, and to take
no account of what is called the "party line." For
each party has its lines, whether general or sec-
ondary—complicated nets outside of which one
would not be able to beat about the bush with im-
punity.

Is such thinking as this peculiar to this season
between spring and autumn, to this muddled
sky, to this lively and fresh breath of an August
denuded of torpor and which keeps the spirit on
the lookout? Or is it simply my share of man's age-
old dream that man should face man without prej-
udice, without doctrinaire slogans and hypocrisy
but with only a "pure look"—one which settles
on human beings with that attention from which
love can be born?

Hostile Old Age

I KNOW something about old age: it's already a long time now that I have been frequenting, at the end of a bridge, that antechamber of eternity where the candidates lay siege to the door. It is Charon's bark surrounded by suppliant shades. At my advanced age I have acquired the right, unfortunately, to confess that I hardly believe in the myth of the "beautiful old man," even though I have known some old people whom I dearly loved. Old age is never beautiful, because punishment is never beautiful. There is a species of petrified old man which gives the illusion of beauty; we are impressed by his appearance. . . . But the statue is usually hollow and little men hide within it like the Greeks inside the flanks of the Trojan horse.

21

Handsome octogenarians are automatons at the center of which there is nearly always an alien will. They expel it sometimes with a hiccup of disgust. What is odious in an old man is precisely this alien will which is nothing more than a substitute for the one he has lost! Will I ever forget that sinister spectacle at the Academy during the Occupation? Abel Bonnard, as if stuck to Cardinal Baudrillart's side, never lost sight of him for a second under a state at once imperious and servile. The Prince of the Church was sunk wretchedly in his seat. He who had in the past been a character (and even a bad one . . .) no longer had the strength, nor undoubtedly the desire, to push back this contact and protect his purple robe from it.

An old man loses out on all counts, for he does not even benefit from the numbness of his passions. Young men are purer than old men among whom, all too often, the imagination inherits their lost potency. In truth the grandeur of old age can be only of a spiritual order: a beautiful old man is a saintly one. But they are rarer than one generally imagines because old age is the sum of a life and each one of our acts, the least thought, is found in the end product.

All Souls' Day

A CEMETERY saddens us because it is the only place of the world in which we do not meet our dead again. Everywhere else, we carry them with us. It is enough to close our eyes to feel this breath against our neck, this faithful hand on our shoulder. The house, the garden, also remember: my mother's easy chair still sags under her weight; the fabric looks worn where she used to rest her elbows. Our familiar universe multiplies around us the images of those who continue to live within us.

At the cemetery, we believe that it is necessary to turn away from our own hearts where the dead are living, and to seek them outside us, on the earth, in the earth, where what already was not there completes its dissolution. For a corpse is essentially an absence, an abandoned, rejected thing—mortal remains at last. A feeling of trickery enters into the hideous dismay which we experience at the spectacle of death: our loved one is there and is no longer there. He has escaped from himself and in his flight he leaves this part of his being between our arms, the only visible and tangible part, which nevertheless no longer resembles him—the only part perhaps, unfortunately, that we knew how to love.

But if this flesh, hardly become cold, had already become a stranger to us, how much more so must be a chiseled stone over that which no longer has a name in any human language! And we remain standing there, the poor living, at the edge of these excavations where, for those who do not know how to pray, no gesture imposes itself on any other. They hold their hats in their hand, lay flowers on the grave, straighten out a wreath, give a thought to the fact that the grill needs repainting. Here the basest expression takes on a tragic meaning: they don't know just what kind of a long face to pull.

Even those who pray and who have the power to introduce the dead into all the religious acts of their

life, attain less easily to this reunion before a sepulcher where, despite themselves, images of corruption and annihilation take the place of the familiar aspect of those whom they have lost. No, it
is not around the stone that covers them that our
dead hasten to if we call them. But what Christian,
after communion, has not seen their tender or grave
faces appear, one by one—as if the little host burning inside him drew them out of the darkness; as
if they wanted to break this bread with their sur-
viving son, to have a part in this marvel. And we
recognize even the grandfather who disappeared
during our childhood, and of whom we barely remember a word, an attitude; and even this father
carried off in the floodtide of youth of whom we
have preserved no memory. And we confuse them
with no other, we are sure of their identity. Perhaps this woman who has lost a very small child,
whom probably she alone has mourned, does not
experience the slightest shadow of a doubt before
this visage that smiles at her, the visage of her son
grown up and flowered in God. And behind those
most near, we have the presentiment of an avid and
silent throng—triumphant? Sorrowing? We do not
know. But they invade our being, at this minute

after communion; they live in us, gathered around Him Who loved them as He loved us.

Have we ever been witnesses of this silent and sweet coming of those who have preceded us in peace, before their graves? No, without a doubt. But perhaps it is not in order to find them that we must carry out this pilgrimage. After we have bowed over these remains, let us recall what our belief is on this subject, our immense hope. In the *Credo*, we affirm our faith in the resurrection of the flesh. The resurrection of the flesh . . . who of us ever lets his thought rest on it? We would per-haps tremble with joy if this faith were living in us. A cemetery is indeed the place where those of us who have preserved it must dare to contemplate our hope.

How many have preserved it in the Christian family? What is the position of the different Chris-tian Churches today in regard to this dogma? Is it an illusion? It seems that even among ourselves, our attention is drawn less gladly to this point than to others. Job, whose body was consumed and whose bone cleaved to his skin, and who had nothing but lip around his teeth, cries out, "For I know that my

Redeemer liveth, and in the last day I shall rise out of the earth, and I shall be clothed again with my skin, and in my flesh I shall see my God. . . ." Yet I know men whom this inconceivable certitude does not disconcert but whom it fills with light: hardly does the fog of their youths lift and their poor agitated strivings toward happiness abate than they have a presentiment that the answer to the enigma of human suffering consists entirely in this exultation of the holy man Job. Likewise, when I was a child and tears came to my eyes upon reading about the misfortunes of the hero, my brother would reassure me: "Don't cry . . . I can swear to you that the story comes out all right in the end. . . ."

Nevertheless, let us not be misled in our hope: if what we have loved of creatures is this very corruption which will not be born again, we must remain with our sadness. These looks of passion, this burning hand that sought ours, none of that will be restored to us. St. Paul attests to us: "What is sown in corruption rises in incorruption. What is sown in dishonor rises in glory; what is sown in weakness rises in power. What is sown in a natural body rises in a spiritual body." The mourning of volup-tuousness therefore is the only one which cannot await consolation. Even, unfortunately, when it does not seem criminal, human love is often but the encounter of two weaknesses. In the creature we attach ourselves to what is perishable, to what passes. And our awareness of this increases our tenderness. This alteration, this uninterrupted de-struction of the beloved being, renews our love and maintains it through suffering. Thus the romantic poet invites us to love what we shall never see twice: *"Ah! qui verra deux fois ta grâce et ta tendresse...."*

This part of the beloved being will never be re-stored to us, and it would be absurd to believe that we shall regret it on the day among days when the mortal body of the beloved will be clothed in im-mortality: any sadness is inconceivable in the king-dom of perfect joy. In this thought, perhaps we will find a new reason to weep on this day. We cannot do otherwise, we who are not saints.

When his sister Jacqueline died, Pascal, undoubt-edly, was numbered among those persons about whom Mlle. des Vertus wrote, "They too were at death's door." Nevertheless he gave no sign of this, asking only the grace of so saintly a death for himself and repeating, "Blessed are those who die and who die thus in the Lord." This stiffness does not suit us. Would He, who wept over His friend Lazarus at the very instant that He was about to resuscitate him, exact it from us? But we, we can only snatch our Lazaruses from the limbo of oblivion and for only a very short time.... Let us weep then with those who have no hope, but let them not be the same tears. In his great book, *The Degrees of Knowledge*, Jacques Maritain poses what he calls the problem of Faust in these terms: "The mystic possession of the very holy God in eternal charity, or the physical possession of a poor flesh in the fugitiveness of time ..." A dilemma, it's true, which nobody here below escapes, but which will be resolved on that day on which, healed of all its wounds, eternally pure and glorious, this poor flesh will also have been restored to us.

Sexagesima Sunday

THERE is no page in world literature which surpasses the verses in the Epistles to the Corinthians which are read today at the Mass. Paul confides all his secrets to us as if they were snatched from him: "Who is weak, and I am not weak? Who is made to stumble, and I am not inflamed?" Everything is said up to the moment of ecstasy, up to the mysterious words heard fourteen years before, but also up to that thorn in the flesh which tortured him, up to that angel of Satan who buffeted him.

This overwhelming love of Paul for his brothers, which still kindles us after so many centuries, obliges us to question ourselves on our incurable wickedness. Gide often posed the question: "Why do Catholics have such a harsh bite?" It is true that

Louis Veuillot, that Léon Bloy, that Bernanos wrote bitingly. It is not for his gentleness that Claudel will get to see The One in whom he believed. I don't think that coincidence and chance play a role here. Religious discipline, sacramental life, in a word the state of grace, preserves and liberates in the faithful a force, an increase of power which in the majority of men the passions confiscate to their advantage. And it is the hunger and thirst for justice in all orders of being that benefit therefrom—this exigency which keeps silent in us in times of forlornness and sin. How could it subsist in the hearts of so many men who agree that for them nothing counts in the world save gratification? Bernanos above all and Claudel: two privileged cases to observe this state of exuberance, these safety valves of a powerful and strongly contained organization. Perhaps it is because of this trait, for His violence, that Christ, in so far as He is a man, most resembles us. If He had been an invented personage, He would have been shown to us as someone suave and easygoing. But He overflows with indignation, He points with His finger, He denounces. He will not rest until He has this pack of Pharisees arrayed against Him. His holy fury stirs up the executioners of whom He will have need for His suffering and torment.

Yes, that is the beautiful side of our rages. But I discern another one which is less flattering: this is the incredible pleasure that the piece written with verve and in one sitting, which has hardly escaped from one's hands, quivers in the target, while the spectators utter "Oh's" and "Ah's." But the target is a living one, Mr. Christian. Your cause is just? Granted. X and Y deserve to be hauled over the coals? Yes, they deserve to be hauled over the coals. But you should not be so happy over it. Brotherly correction should not entail any pleasure in the brother who administers it. It is amazing that Pascal never reproached himself for having written *Les Provinciales*, not even on his deathbed. I would have been more scrupulous than Pascal on this point. I would not have dissembled the extreme pleasure taken in writing them, with the aggravating circumstance that he hated the Molinists from the bottom of his heart, when it is an understatement to say that I don't at all hate my "enemies" (to speak only of the last battle, I have always loved Paulhan as much as one can love a Chinese, but after a certain trick which he played on us I feel I have the right to pull his pigtail a little).

33

See How They Love
One Another

THE absurdity of writers who aspire to survive in the memory of men! If they could only foresee what the zeal of their friends will disinter. The faithful friends of a great dead man would have to be taught to forget the ordures. Did the friends of Georges Bernanos believe they were doing a service to his memory by digging up from a merciful oblivion the speech he made to student members of the *Action Française*, in order to publish it in their bulletin, and in which I critically remark the following:

> Nobody will ever let me take the livid mug of [here the name of a Catholic whom one may not love, but who is most worthy of esteem and respect] for the face of an honest man, this kind of

bearded tumor, burned within by all the acidities and all the scum of a poisonous blood. Even if a cardinal places a scarf of the commander of a knightly order around this anatomical fixture . . .

This ordure is dated 1928: Bernanos therefore had already weathered his fortieth year. If the author of the *Diary of a Country Priest* and the *Dialogue of the Carmelites* had written a pornographic work, would you have published it? But there is something even worse here: one Christian publicly spitting on another for the pleasure of making some young lunatics shake with laughter.

Dreams of a Summer Day

AT low tide the sandbanks emerge like the russet and briny backs of the gods who dwell in the depths. Billows of a translucent jade green bestir themselves around these huge, half-sunken bodies. Then, suddenly, the water blackens where it covers over the deep. Only the pine trees, in their tormented stance, remember the assaults they have withstood from the crazy sea at other times. But how calm they are today between the sand and the blue! Each one of them wears a cicada on its bark with which to lull itself to sleep. On the horizon, their mass pressed against the ridge of the pale dunes separates the waters and the sky.

The tanned young bodies bending and straightening up, and chasing after each other at the bottom of my terrace, have the same color as the sandbanks:

they seem to be made of the same flesh as these gods asleep on the unruffled sea. They laugh, full of innocence and joy: I gaze upon and I contemplate this perfect day, but they are living it. Already this day appears to me as it will linger in their memory when I shall have returned to dust. It is the privilege of the poet that he no longer has need of time to effect this transmutation of a present, still confused and disordered, into a radiant remembrance.

They will say to their children: "It was in July 1960. . . . We were staying at the Villa Saint-Dominique where Gabriel D'Annunzio once lived. What a lot of male and female cousins we were in the old chalet which had the smell of varnished toys about it! Ramblers embraced the trunks of the pine trees, and big, miraculous dahlias grew in the sand. Summers were beautiful in those days. . . ."

Nothing yet discloses to them the nature of conspiracy between water, land and sky to make children believe that happiness exists. And at the beginning of our decline we ourselves forget what we know, attending to this whispering, to this beating of the waves, to this endless rocking, to this lie which permits us to get our breath back again just before the last lap.

In truth it is we ourselves who lie to ourselves. If there were no human eye to contemplate this horizon, nor ear to listen to the drowsy sea, its murmur would not be a hymn of joy. Appearances contain nothing of a human character save what we ourselves have put in them. All our desires are suspended over this beautiful day like the swarms of bees which suddenly concentrate and thicken around a dead branch. The landscape is naught else but a stretched canvas on which we project our heart. I write "our heart," making no distinction between that of these youthful beings playing and splashing in the water around the pinnaces, and the old, overworked hearts of creatures in their decline. For nothing more resembles the desire for happiness, among adolescents fascinated by all the mirages, than the hunger still suffered by those who from harsh experience know that happiness doesn't exist. Or at least that it exists not like an object that we possess once and forever, like a pearl, or like an incorruptible diamond that we press in our hands.

Happiness! Undoubtedly it sometimes placed its hands on their eyes, it had a face, it was wholly contained in the mysterious gaze over which their foreheads bent; it had its density, its weight, and it

was the weight of a head against their shoulders.
And then it was no longer there. . . . What is happiness which is not always there?

It is five o'clock. The tide has covered over the
sandbanks. The sea is of a paler green there where
the tawny backs of the gods have disappeared. The
setting sun designs a huge fan of light on the sur-
face of the waters. I am reminded of a line which
I read in *Le Soulier de Satin:* "There is nothing for
which man is less made than for happiness and of
which he grows weary so quickly. . . ." Perhaps it
is not happiness that takes flight from us, but we
who flee from it. Is there not an instinct among most
men that drives them to spoil, to destroy, what was
their portion here below, as if through what was
given to them at the outset they were looking for
something else of which they did not know the
name—something which resembles it perhaps and
which, nevertheless, is not that? What our heart
projects on the shadowless blue of this summer
day, or this drowsy sea where the waves form
tongues of foam as small as gulls, is certainly the
desire for happiness, but of a happiness that will
never pass away. "Holy sweets of heaven, adorable
ideas."

Just as the horizon changes from moment to moment, keeping step with this beautiful day as it reaches its plenitude (already the fan of light is being closed again and a full-blown sail traverses it in a few seconds), so is it too the reflection of an ever-changing heart which the seascape throws back at us. What does it matter, sighs a voice, that happiness is essentially something that does not last? For what would we do with a life which would not be tragic? And the tragedy of life is to love what is ephemeral. It would not be any more insane to attach oneself with a desperate heart to this beautiful, dying day than to a creature. Yet this is precisely what every man does from the moment that he begins to love. What madness! But one which gives life a taste so wondrously bitter that nothing less than the love of God is necessary in order for man to renounce this desperation.

"There is nothing for which man is less made than for happiness. . . ." The fact is that a certain suffering, and even a certain despair, are also happiness. Soon, perhaps, we shall grow weary of this somnolent blue, weary of this sea whose slumber is as peaceful as that of a child. The west wind will have to rise and draw this sea out of its drowsiness.

The pine trees will have to shake their tormented crests and spin out the sighing of the demented waters far into the distance, and deep inland. This evening, riddled by the arrows of the sunset (how slowly the sun disappears!), we imagine those overcast days when the spindrifts on our face will have that taste of salt familiar to us since the first tears of our earliest childhood.

The Empty Day

INTERVIEWS, telephone calls, a two-hour rehearsal at six o'clock, still another interview. Now, I am alone. By a miracle the house is silent. I left my own self this morning; this evening I go in search of myself—a thing not easily to be found. The world's tumult prolongs its echo inside me. I still hum with the noise made by a thousand voices. Some faces obsess me, above all those of my interpreters: these faces full of tears in which an imaginary suffering is expressed that I myself have plotted. *My God, where are You? Quite near me, only a stone's throw. But how can I get to You through this crowd of creatures whose phantoms still possess me? How can I hear You amid all this hubbub, You who talk softly?*

It is not enough that I desire it. It would be all too simple to tell You: "Wait for me, I'll be back this evening...." Many do not lose the certitude of Your presence in the world: I believe it, I know it. But there is a world and a world. The pressure of my glittering and full life against the invisible cell in which I seek refuge becomes stronger with each passing day.

That I suffer from it is no great misfortune. But that one quickly habituates himself to doing without You! We have remained children—children who would be free to be always at play, the interminable playtime that is our life.

It is not only against the passions of love that no other remedy exists except flight. The only resource against the dispersion, so to speak, of my days would be to create zones of silence—silence in which to hear the thunders of Your love and to refresh myself on the waters that alone can slake the thirst of the human heart.

The Man-Dog

A T the Buechenwald camp gate stood a niche
for the watchdog. A chained beast barked at
passers-by, and greedily buried its snout in its bowl
of mush. Even though the beast never stood up on
its hind paws, one got the feeling after a while that
it was really a man. And it was!

Among all the agonies invented by these vir-
tuosos of torture, this appears to me as their master-
piece—one which degrades man in his dignity as a
creature, in his resemblance to God. But the strang-
est thing about all this is that the man-dog was not
a Frenchman, nor a Russian, nor a Pole, nor a
Czech, nor a Jew: he was a German, the former
anti-Nazi mayor of Weimar. Since 1933 these
hangmen had reduced him to the condition of a

brute by means of a patient, insatiable cruelty.
Nightmare magicians, they had taken the time to
perfect their sorcery. What successful malefice!
The mayor of Weimar, literally, had become a dog!

I put this question to collaborators, to unregen-
erate Pétainists: What would these Nazis, who
were capable of treating their fellow Germans like
this (for these horror camps were originally planned
for their own political opponents) have done to us
Frenchmen had they been the victors? Even though
the crafty and underhanded destruction of the elite
of France was already in progress, that was still
nothing: we should have known what the Poles,
the anti-Nazi Germans, have learned. Furthermore
we know it, we see it with our eyes. But those who
caress the faces of these Lazaruses barely returned
from hell, alas, touch it with their very hands.

We who pleaded for you, and who protested
that you had been led astray by the ringleaders of
the Vichy swindle, that your good faith had been
taken by surprise, do we not have the right to expect that you should beat your breasts in penance?
The triumph of your political policy would have
ended in the collapse of France, and her fall into
shame. You see this clearly enough now, and what

have you to answer, except insults? But acknowl-
edge first of all that Nazism, which you found so
praiseworthy, has lowered man quite beyond the
level of a beast, for the mayor of Weimar become a
dog is less horrible than those who reduced him to
this state. A dog for all that is still a creature of
God. But the lovers of lamp shades made of human
skin revive the old Manichaean leaven in me and
force me to fight against the temptation to believe
that there is an accursed part in us and that some
Other than Our Father in heaven conceived this
murderous and sanguinary world.

England and France

WE know very well that politics is not a matter of sentiment. But that does not prevent
sentiment—that is, the exploitation of feelings—
from playing a fundamental part in politics. At the
very moment that she was striking at Germany in
the air and on the seas, indeed on the very day after
Mers-el-Kebir, England won an even swifter victory over French hearts: "This is London calling!
Turn your radio set low . . ."

I recall the drawing room where the German
officer, who slept on the first floor, might have
barged in at any moment, the meager fire over
which we popped corn. Never for a moment did
I lose the sensation of the frozen landscape around
us, of my country straitened by shame in the silence

of the winter nights. Then, suddenly, that voice, those commingled French and English voices: "Nothing is finished. On the contrary everything is beginning. The Allies need you, your confidence, your loyalty . . ." Even before the Gestapo was unmasked, before the blood of the first hostages had been shed, our humiliation, our hatred of the occupying army, everything within us became a party to that love which that indomitable nation inspired in us, "a free land amid dark seas." Even when her sons brought us death and destruction, we could see in them only the sons of a country which had not allowed itself to be enslaved and which had promised to wrest us from slavery one day. I remember the first attack on the Renault factories and on Saint-Cloud. The planes roared by practically at the level of our rooftop in Auteuil. The feeling that ceaselessly kept drawing us back to the windows was less one of curiosity at a terrifying spectacle, than one of happiness at seeing free men in our skies.

Nothing can keep this feeling from gripping us still, nor this love from living on within us. To the politicians who pride themselves on being most realistic, we repeat: Feeling is also a fact, and love is also a datum, a creative element. Economic determinism is not the only factor that plays a role. The frightful misunderstandings in Syria or elsewhere change nothing of the bond that unites us English and French—namely a certain conception of man, his condition, his fate—as we cross the threshold of this frightful, unknown world. Both Englishmen and Frenchmen have a common task: to lift man, fallen so low in abjection and crime, and to restore him to the dignity of a being created in the image of God the Father.

English friends, believe me: the pre-condition for the salvation of Europe depends on our spiritual brotherhood. Twenty years of Fascism and Nazism have failed to destroy, either in Italy or Germany, the leaven of the Word which will never pass away. In Germany Catholic bishops and Protestant pastors have always known that they had to fight Evil incarnate in their own country. It will have been of no use to have defeated this Satanic dictatorship if our joint effort did not restore life to its victim: the human spirit—the spirit which for a quarter of a century has been ferociously subjected to the State, the Race, Technology. To be sure, the spirit has been freed, but it has been contaminated and defiled by its servitude. Now the responsibility for healing this spirit lies in our feeble hands. Let us never compromise this healing. Let politics never deflect us from this sacred task.

The Dream of the Wise Men

IN ruined Stuttgart I recalled something Anatole
France had said in 1903 at Tréguier in a speech
before the statue of Ernest Renan: "Slowly but con-
stantly humanity realizes the dreams of the sages."
One of Renan's favorite dreams was that one day a
small number of scientists would hold the secret of
destroying the planet, and that therefore the rest
of mankind would be compelled to obey them.
Now he can clearly see that if humanity realizes
the dreams of the wise men, it does so not without
adding a few sinister retouchings.

It is true that American laboratories have perfected their methods to the point where the last
city razed was destroyed in twenty-three minutes.
An optimist might conclude that Renan was a good

prophet and that the scientists will in fact have the last word—and that they will have it all the better since there will be nobody left to answer them. But Renan and his disciple France were very naïve to believe (or maybe they just feigned to believe it) that the secrets of matter would be held only by good and virtuous men. Why should not even evil men be good experimenters? If in the course of annihilation the laboratories of the Third Reich have been conquered by those of the United States, they nevertheless did some pretty good work first themselves: the furious madmen were very able chemists, and they were the first to dare experimenting on human guinea pigs. The son of a friend of ours was shipped to Buechenwald and marked with initials which stood for *Nacht und Nebel* (night and fog): this meant that he was consigned to German researchers who had received permission to use and abuse his young body. But on the eve of his arrival the laboratory where he was destined to finish his life (with what suffering!) was blown up by a bomb perfected in New York. Thus the dream of the mad German, luckily for our friend, was spoiled by that of the Anglo-Saxon sage.

But the worst of it is that it is not just the criminally insane and the virtuous wise men who arm themselves against one another with terrifying inventions. It is not simply a question of a duel to the death between good men and bad. Could Renan and France have really believed that the wise men would never devour each other? The will to power of empires, which is an irrepressible instinct because it is impersonal and anonymous and results from laws over which individuals have no control, does not recoil before any of the means furnished to it by scientific researchers. Undoubtedly these are bitter thoughts, but salutary. In 1903 the contemporaries of Anatole France were like the sleepwalker who, singing, runs along the edge of a roof. We have been terribly awakened. At Beuchenwald, at Auschwitz, at Ravensbrueck, at Dachau, we have seen just how far man can go in ferocity, and to what an extent, alas, he has the power to debase his brothers by depriving them of bread. Humanity has been awakened forever, but it has also been unmasked. And it has given up deceiving itself. There are too many fine phrases with which our fathers beguiled themselves which we no longer dare to pronounce, and henceforth the victorious nations can no longer have recourse to the old diplomatic language in order to conceal what is contrary to the old beautiful words.

We know what remains—what word, what hope. It is still the same, and after nearly two thousand years, the only one which resists all the denials of destiny. Hence even the least Christian among us is tempted to repeat the prayer of the two pilgrims on the road to Emmaus to the Stranger on the threshold of the humble inn: "Stay with us for it is getting towards evening, and the day is now far spent . . ."

Nacht und Nebel

IN the last essay I made reference to the initials for *Nacht und Nebel*—night and fog—which in the concentration camps designated a class of boys to be used as guinea pigs in scientific experiments. Thus marked, these unfortunates could be "cut up at pleasure." . . . An anonymous correspondent informs me (am I, perhaps, the only one who did not know it?) that in Wagner's *The Ring of the Nibelungs, Nacht und Nebel* are the first words of Alberich's incantation which, when he wore his helmet, enabled him to disappear, being replaced by a column of fog. "At Buechenwald," added my correspondent, "they tried to make the spell come true."

These Germans will never stop surprising us. It

is not so much their cruelty which is astonishing, even though it is beyond all measure. After all, cruelty is the best shared thing in the world; every people has its own manner of ferocity: here burnings are carried on more artfully than elsewhere, and there lynchings are conducted in a manner superior to anywhere else. There are specialties in torture, styles particular to each nation. But the Germans beat us all by applying mass-production methods to murder, and singularly to the destruction of an entire race, by research in the scientific yield of torture, by the rationalization of crime, and a certain manner of allying the gratification of the sadist with the experimentation of the scientist. This is now recognized by everyone in the world, and their pre-eminence in this field henceforth will never be questioned. Nevertheless, the Wagnerian origin of the phrase *Nacht und Nebel* opens, for me at least, a new perspective on the German abyss, and therefore on the human abyss, for after all, the Germans are human beings.

I had always believed that in the artist, in the poet above all, in the musician—and in every man worthy of understanding them—there was an integral purity like a secret and preserved innocence

58

of childhood, no matter how guilty they might have been, even under a pile of sins accumulated over a lifetime, even after committing the most deplorable acts. The defilements of a Baudelaire, a Verlaine, a Rimbaud, are covered over by this night of inspiration, by this fog of dreams: *Nacht und Nebel* ... One might also say that these shadows and this mist purify them.

I know a Mozart lover who, during these dreadful four years, could not bear to hear one of the recordings which formerly helped to keep him alive, because he felt that the abyss between that celestial music and an epoch dedicated to murder was too great to be breached. In his eyes divine art no longer had anything in common with criminal life. For the Germans, on the contrary, during these same years music and poetry inspired crime. Wagner rose from his grave to collaborate with the hangman, and the cry of the slaughtered victim became a note in the symphony.

This is just one sign among thousands of the total subversion of the German spirit. And I ponder—how does one treat this strange and monstrous patient? Abel, what are you going to do with your brother Cain? I am wondering about our personal attitude, the manner in which each of us on his own count deals with "the German problem." As for the attitude of the great victorious empires and their policy toward the vanquished . . . let us hope that they will not retreat into their respective zones, each determined to exploit it and fortify themselves there with God knows what ulterior motives! If this should happen an odious burst of laughter will rise from the shadows and the fog—*Nacht und Nebel*—which enshroud destroyed Germany, and a voice, perhaps Hitler's, or that of the eternal enemy of man, will cry out: "I have succeeded, all the same!"

The Last Act

THIS last act never ends; it is the most difficult to conceive and to describe even when the playwright is God, destiny, or history. If Shakespeare lives, now is the time for him to get to work: the drama is already disengaging itself from the bloody chaos of circumstances. The setting grows smaller hour by hour, since Europe and indeed the whole world is like that piece of paper in the fireplace at whose edges the flames are licking greedily.

I can imagine Shakespeare's stage directions: "Enter General Eisenhower, followed by his victorious army (flourish of trumpets)" or: "The hall of a castle in Bavaria. Laval, Déat, Brinon, Darnand, Bonnard, are yelping like dogs around the somnolent old Marshal: "We must leave, *M. le Maréchal,* time is pressing . . ." But the old man is not listening; he has never been in a hurry to make his departures. He is talking to himself: "They say I am a criminal because I stopped the war, and that Hitler is a criminal because he continues it. I don't understand . . ."

For that matter, did he ever understand? Perhaps he was less desperate than we thought. He is sure to have defenders before the bar of history as long as there are certain elements of the French middle class for whom he embodied a political ideal: a well-ordered society with each one in his place where, behind the impressive and paternal old Head of State a handful of powerful men (but less powerful than the police who protect them) control the State; where the good worker, satisfied with his lot, talks to you hat in hand and one calls him "my friend," and where the only unforgivable crime is that against acquired wealth and the established order. The sad thing is that it required a foreign occupation to make the French nation pretend to submit to this happiness.

It would be interesting to know just how each of the men surrounding the old Marshal got themselves into this fatal fix of having this only choice between a frontier post and a lamppost. "Laval or the clumsiness of the skillful" . . . We have all seen this phenomenon in smaller animals. With Bonnard, it was less ambition that played a role than an insatiable passion for politics. Perhaps because I never met Déat, his case strikes me as the most mysterious. A very intelligent man who was a socialist in normal school, he openly detested and distrusted Vichy. But he believed in and adhered to National-Socialism in so far as doctrine (with the accent on socialism). In any case, not one of these unfortunates has the stature of a Shakesperian hero, not by a long shot. Only Hitler belongs to the category of genius, and he is already the victim of his own legend. Or rather his history discourages legend: for in the centuries to come what will imagination add to what is known of Auschwitz, Buechenwald and Ravensbrueck, whose unimaginable horrors have been unveiled by witnesses of the stature of Julien Cain, and Professor Richet! Who will tell us the story of the last nights of Hitler? Perhaps a single death conceals from him those millions of human beings of whom he was the executioner; perhaps, from among all these corpses, it is the bloody shroud of Roehme, his murdered friend, who rises up, opens his mouth and, in the name of that immense throng of martyrs, cries out to him like the ghosts in *Richard III:* "Fainting despair; despairing yield thy breath!"

Europe

FRANKLIN ROOSEVELT was one of the few leaders to think in terms of "Europe." We no longer dared even to pronounce the name of Europe during the four long years under the Nazi yoke. Our temporary conquerors had defiled everything, even words, and even that word laden with the richest human meaning and associations. When a Frenchman came and said, "I'm a European first of all . . ." we knew that this meant: "I have chosen to be a traitor." What the Germans called Europe was a chain gang, a chain of nations riveted to one another and toiling for the master race to the point of exhaustion.

Today the hunted overlords wander among the rubble and stumble over the corpses of their sons.

The Nazi Reich no longer comes between our thought and the true face of old Europe. That face has been disfigured forever. Man has destroyed with his own hands the highest testimonials to his own dignity. We remember the ship of which France was the figurehead, and the spirit common to all the peoples who made up the crew. Then Voltaire addressed himself to all minds, Rousseau released the same wellspring of tears in every heart, Kant posed the problem of human knowledge for all human thought. When barricades were raised in Paris, all the capitals of the world trembled. Nietzsche learned about man in Stendhal and in all our moralists, Frenchmen met at Weimar in Goethe's house, and at Bayreuth on the hill of Parsifal. Then, convulsed with joy, we heard Bruno Walter conduct Mozart's *Don Giovanni* at Salzburg.

The delights of the privileged, would you say? No, not at all, for even the most humble had a share in this culture. The very air we breathed was laden with intelligence, the landscapes were ennobled by the eyes of the painters and poets who had contemplated them. It is this, or rather the little that remains of it, that we want to preserve. Today all human genius is pivoted around the machine. Men, fallen into childhood, build extraordinary mechanical toys. They are very proud of them, admire how well they work, and they mass-produce them in no time, indeed in less time than it takes to raze a town. After which, every great empire will be equipped to rebuild a Europe of concrete and sheet iron for itself, and inundate it with manufactured goods until there are no outlets left so that once again the factories, equipped in accordance with the latest technological progress, will perfect "the bloody machinery of destruction."

This is the bloody, really vicious circle from which we have to try to save what remains of "Europe." Are we going to surrender to the obsession with our decadence, our smallness? Behold the return of the time when the earth was peopled with giants: it is the hour of the human hero, the hour of the creature having the modest proportions of a man.

Spiritual Conflict

DURING the last hours of the war one would have said that men, blinded by blood, were hesitating at the edge of peace as if it were the last trick of destiny. "Funny kind of a peace," a pessimist had whispered in my ear, "which is announced by the same sirens which only yesterday made us shake with fear." But we are not pessimists. The illusions of 1918 did us too much harm for us to dread the lucidity to which we are condemned. It is not enough just to see things clearly, to be sure! Cassandra could not save Troy. Nevertheless one must first see the situation clearly.

In *Antony and Cleopatra* in the scene where Lepidus disappears (he was one of the "Big Three" of Rome) and Antony and Octavius are left face to face, Enobarbus pronounces some words from which one never ends trying to extract the essence: "Then, world, thou hast a pair of chaps [jaws], no more."

Let me be clearly understood. We are not, thank God, afraid of being pulverized between our Anglo-Saxon friends and our Russian friends. It is simply that we would like to see them get on with each other better than they do. It is not the clash of two political programs that disturbs us, nor is it the conflict of interests, either. Two ethics are grappling with each other, two different views of man confront each other. This is the truth of the matter.

Undoubtedly we cannot expect that any empire will voluntarily submit to any other law save that of its interests and its growth. But in every empire this law is usually more or less countered by the spiritual heritage of the great philosophers of antiquity and of the Gospel. This is the root of the misunderstanding between our Allies. I know quite well that the assiduous reading of the Bible has not prevented the British Empire from always having at its head statesmen of whom the least one can say is that on every occasion they have shown themselves to be exceedingly realistic. But even the most tough-minded of them had always to reckon, in their policies, with that old puritan England, with her exacting soul, and her uncompromising morality.

I seriously doubt that Mr. Khrushchev knows this sort of difficulty; perhaps he even finds it hard to believe that it exists for others. Thus the Polish revolt or the German revolt or the Hungarian revolt, which are serious in their own right, has dimensions of which it would be a good thing for us to be aware. The conflict is of a spiritual order and it goes infinitely beyond those which the chancelleries of this world are accustomed to regulating.

2

For a moment those who, despite their convictions and passionate foregone conclusions, in their hearts preserved a profound concern for French unity had some hope of a relaxation of tension. There was a promise of appeasement in the air we breathed. A Council of Ministers had decided to delay investigations then in course. At last a feeble light was indicating the way out of the labyrinth. But suddenly we found ourselves set in the administration of day-to-day justice. No one pronounced a word of civic peace, as if our leaders were resigned to living forever with this maturating wound in the side of France, and France were condemned forever to the rot of hospital wards.

The reason for this falling back into the old rut was clearly visible to everyone: the Allied advance in Germany suddenly became a descent into hell. We knew that these concentration camps existed. But there is a great gap between hearing and seeing. We have seen with our own eyes, heard with our own ears, the witnesses of the most extensive outrage which the dignity of man has ever suffered since there have been men on earth who killed each other. All this has revived or exacerbated the anger directed against those Frenchmen who collaborated with the authors and accomplices of these crimes, and who had hoped for their victory. Undoubtedly, the municipal elections have been influenced by these disclosures. Ill luck would have it that the return of the old man of Silmaringen should coincide with the reawakening of this all too legitimate indignation. Thus we found ourselves engaged more deeply than ever in a domestic conflict in which neither of the two parties would give an inch.

For it would have been useless to entertain illusions: facts are powerless against a *mystique*, a myth. On the contrary they reinforce it: I received printed prayers, strange pamphlets in which General de Gaulle was invited to come and kneel and beat his breast before the crematory ovens of Buechenwald. This no longer aroused anger or scorn; it was a wound which one probes, the depths of which have not been gauged.

The politicians, who are far from wanting a reconciliation and who, on the contrary, await the extermination of their adversaries from this struggle, may rejoice over this state of things. Although we ourselves are quite capable of passionate foregone conclusions, everything dissuades us from yielding to them; not only the law of love in which we believe and which stands above every other law, but also the interests of France which are our most obvious and pressing concern. It is useless to dwell on this; it is strikingly obvious at the first examination. Let us remember, nevertheless, that this lacerated France struggles with herself in the middle of a world in dissolution in which she occupies a corner of an immense battlefield. Her history is merely the history of a province. Meanwhile the victors take each other's measure on the ruins of the German Third Reich.

I certainly agree with Claude Morgan that it is not only frivolous but indecent to indulge in pleasantries such as: "Will the war between the Big Three take place?" Perhaps the diplomats and businessmen will not be able to reconcile their divergent interests. What seems serious is not so much the latent or overt conflicts of interest here and there on this planet. More serious still is the evidence of two human groupings, at once allies and antagonists, who have different ideas concerning mankind, and different conceptions of history; each of whom, furthermore, has a morality that holds the morality of the other in ridicule.

The Native's Return

AFTER two years to the day I had come back to my old house which I was forced to leave in a hurry after a warning by the Resistance. The scene of my agony stood unchanged under a somber sky though a storm was on the prowl. The immense horizon, which had twice appeared to me to shrink in the expectation of war, was spread far and wide. *The vermin, the thousands of worms who gnawed at you, have been exterminated and you are still there, beloved earth!* In celebration of my return the vines offered me the most bountiful harvest of grapes that I had seen since my childhood. The storm, at once feared and desired, brought only the rain which the grapes needed in order not to wither away.

75

On my table I found the open book and the interrupted letter as I had left them, as well as issues of the *Nouvelle Revue Française*, edited by the unfortunate Drieu. What would he have had to say on what I reread in the light of the judgment of God who had chosen between us! What was striking was that some of those comrades who went astray, the Drieu in particular, started from an idea that was at once just and corrupt. They felt strongly that the concept of nationhood, in the narrow sense which French Jacobins gave it, was done for and that events would set their curse upon it. Their irreparable error, in a moral and political sense, was to give their hearts and their consent to an Hitlerian Europe, to an order assured by crime, to bondage to crime incarnated in one man. The moral error was that they said Yes to the theoreticians of the brutal attack: to racists who did not recoil before the destruction of a whole race, to the inventors of a system of repression which, with the precision of clockwork, already raged through all of Germany. (Here I came across an issue of *Match*, dated September 7, 1939, with photographs of Dachau and Buechenwald which we then, perhaps, took to be exaggerated propaganda. It's the same humanity of innocent convicts, wearing the sinister pajamas which are now so familiar, and already dying by the hundreds, every day.)

The political error of those comrades gone astray was their belief that a Germany, in bondage to a gang of adventurers, could impose her will on the Anglo-Saxon world. They did not understand just how relative and limited her power was. Nor did they understand that the pact between the Germans and the Slavs could only be a truce. They were mistaken. At what point did they lose their sense of the possible? The same people who had faith in Doriot inside France, had faith in Germany outside France.

Thus did I muse in the old house that had been restored to me. But a deep layer of emotion reigned under these clear ideas, like a sad happiness: an acquiescence without bitterness to death. For the first time since the Liberation I had hope for the continuity of my country, my race, my family. My youngest son, who was passing by in his rookie's uniform with the vintagers, would still be here when I was gone. I would not be the one to counsel him to go elsewhere, to go for instance to the tropics or elsewhere in search of freedom as so

77

many had done. Freedom was again here! May this beloved earth, on which as children we used to sleep at siesta time, open one day and close again tenderly over our sleep, over this repose which we shall have well deserved.

The Demon of Spain

I REMEMBER having dined at the house of a Spanish grandee, a true El Greco model, during the last days of the monarchy. His beautiful eyes, darkened with fury, observed the representative of a foreign power who, whiskey glass in hand, was talking too loud and whose drunken laugh split his brick-red face in two. "When I think," whispered the Spaniard to me under his breath, "that those people consider us to be monkeys! Why, look at that pompous fool! His people are about to slaughter each other here, but do they have any consideration for Spain? There is not a single nation more misunderstood, more disdained by those Teutons,

79

Anglo-Saxons, and Slavs who, under different words, have never adored anything save force at the service of matter."

My Spanish friend was right, for his country has never counted for much in foreign eyes. She has always been alien and enigmatic to them, and never, perhaps, more of a stranger than when the battle of nations was being fought on her body. She was being trampled underfoot by Gentiles incapable of entering into her mystery. Those Russians, those Italians, those Germans, had come to her ransacked house in order to settle a quarrel that did not concern her, and her own martyrdom remained a mystery to them.

Leaders on both sides trafficked with her and both sides delivered her to wolves who pretended to be devouring each other, but who in reality were devouring themselves. They were playing their game miles away from their own homes. What a marvelous field for maneuvers! they thought. What an unexpected firing range! They were trying out their tanks and torpedoes on the trampled body of Spain, and enjoying themselves immensely. They could with considerable justice be accounted the descendants of those great men among the ancients who made use of their slaves in order to experiment with poisons.

The Spanish people, at once the most carnal and the most spiritual, in whom every idea is incarnated, in whose hearts the spume of divine love and of human passion swirls together, had become the prey of what seemed to be most hostile to its genius: it was being murdered in the name of systems of which it could not even conceive. For at bottom the people of that nation, whose calcinated rock separates hell from heaven, have never been poised in any way except between sanctity and anarchy. And on the nations arrayed in a circle around its martyrdom it darted the frightened and furtive look of the bull, covered with blood, which no longer knows what people want from it.

It could not be said that the right hand of the demon, to whom Spain had been surrendered, did not know what the left hand was doing: did the protagonists of this civil war doubt that in each camp it was the same spirit that moved them, that hurled them one against the other? That spirit was, to be sure, alien to them; for Spain has her demon —one who belongs only to her, cruel and sad, enamored of blood and of death, but he is not the one who had been tearing her apart for months. Spain was agonized, devoured by a sordid demon. The masters of Moscow and of Berlin could trample upon this people like a grape harvest under the wine press; but they could never possess it from within. They could rule over it by virtue of the left fist or through the power of the right fist. But they could never bring down the secret "castle" of the Spanish soul where the drama that is played surpasses that of the distribution of wealth, escapes the categories of the time and re-echoes in eternity.

Heaven on Earth

"THERE has been talk about a dangerous drift leading directly to war," declared the British Prime Minister in the House of Commons. "An Anglo-Soviet war is simply unthinkable. . . ." We had not yet finished squeezing the delicious juice out of these words when tanks rumbled in the streets of Berlin, crowds were machine-gunned in Bizerte, and Khrushchev rattled more rockets. May the British Prime Minister excuse me, but how can we find the testimony of our eyes "unthinkable"?

War is a sickness whose symptoms vary. All the same you would not want it to assume the same form when allied nations come to grips with one another, as when open and declared enemies go at each other's throat. War between allies necessarily assumes a larval aspect. It is nevertheless a war, and one no less costly in human lives. But its secret procedures perhaps make it more dreadful than the open hostilities which it announces and prepares.

If we were to ask a simple soul to suggest a cure for such a tragic situation, no doubt he would ask the masters of the world to take pity on all peoples. But pity is a feeling quite foreign to determinists whose vocation it is to interpret the blind laws of history correctly. To them the pity which soothes the bad conscience of the "haves," and helps them to resign themselves to the inequalities of the human condition, is suspect. Anatole France, who considered himself a socialist and wanted to give two courses to life—irony and pity—died without realizing that thereby he was testifying to sentiments which are hardly worthy of what we nowadays call an "engaged" writer. To all our other privileges of a cultivated middle class, pity adds that of convincing ourselves that we have a beautiful soul. True. But as a character in Dostoevski says somewhere: "Come, come, my friend, one cannot live absolutely without pity. . . ."

After all, the masters of our destiny are men, they have even been children. Vigny wrote in his

Journal that it is difficult to imagine Robespierre as
a baby being carried to his mother by his nurse to
whom the mother smiles and coos, "What a pretty
little baby!" This, however, did not prevent the Incorruptible from being insensitive—far from it!
This first-born of Rousseau shed blood and tears in
like quantities. His imitators today, I fear, have lost
the taste for being moved to pity. A cool head is
now required to observe the concatenation of his-
toric phenomena, so as to become the beneficiaries
thereof. It is certain, for example, that the fruits of
colonialism have come to full maturity, which is a
trump card in Russia's game. She too is a colonialist
in her own way, but of little neighboring peoples
whom she has under her thumb. On the other hand
she does not have distant empires, long exploited
and oppressed, on her hands, where she finds it very
easy to sow the wind in order that others may reap
the whirlwind.

The masters of our fate also think of man, to be
sure. When they consider the future they pose
problems of production; in their dreams they com-
bine industrial might and manpower. Manpower,
productivity . . . Here at last is the beginning and
the end of the materialist conception of the world:

the whole future of the human being just as it was his past, as the Pyramids attest. It is true that not so much sweat and blood will be shed for despots, castes or oligarchies (at least the optimists are free to persuade themselves of this), but for the collective good which, in these blessed times, will be indistinguishable from Europe. The human ants will have the consolation of sacrificing themselves to what is called an "order."

Order, unfortunately, is not always synonymous with happiness. Emmanuel Berl, referring to the Mongols of the great Genghis Khan in his *History of Europe*, cites the judgment of Léon Cahun: "It was not Mongol disorder which was terrifying, rather it was the excess of order. Everywhere they passed they left their mark with three words: *Yassa* (regulation); *Yamei* (office); *Yam*, the frontier station where they stamped passports." History is certainly monotonous. In all epochs, between the massacres and the slaughters, somehow or other miserable human beings have always had to queue up. Oh patience of the poor, who will ever exhaust you?

86

The Evening Stroll

AT the end of a day's work when I allow myself the reward of leaning on the rail of the terrace at the Palais de Chaillot, I succumb to the strange and poignant charm of a city that survives, a charm which in the past belonged only to perishable bodies. It is the fragility of the dome of the Invalides, suspended in the spring twilight and haloed with gold among the clouds, that moves me. What a miracle that this bubble still swells intact above the roofs and the fog!

> *Aimons ce que jamais on ne verra deux fois.*
> *Ah! qui verra deux fois ta grâce et ta tendresse.**

* Let us love what we shall never see twice.
  Ah! who will twice see your grace and tenderness!

It is not only to the ephemeral creature that we dare to dedicate these lines of Vigny, but to the city, more human than any human, to this unspeakably beautiful face composed of trees and stones, the dim river, and these ancient parapets on which we leaned in our youth in the homecomings of early dawn.

The danger of this kind of contemplation is that it engenders a hatred and a fear of change. In the midst of a world turned upside down, France risks succumbing to the dangerous pleasure of finding herself still herself, of being enchanted with her own visage, and sinking into the complacent immobility of Narcissus.

Each time I return to the house and the park where I spent my school holidays, every tree is familiar as is every turn in the walk. Only a few pine trees have died of old age. But if I leave the garden I enter a strange country which does not recognize me: woodcutters and fires have made a desert where once stretched a magic forest. It's as if the house and garden of my childhood had been transported to another planet. Likewise, at the very frontiers of our old France we no longer recognize anything.

88

I do not know if, as André Siegfried wrote, nations have ages. But one thing is certain: some have finished growing, while others continue to dig their roots and their branches under the ground and in the air. For us who have passed the age of growth the problem will be to survive, to persevere in being among these children who are strangers to fatigue and who have the appetite of a wolf, to endure among the great adolescent empires.

The Symptom

THE debate on the laws of charity and those of
justice, which it was believed had been closed
but which is being resumed here and there, resembles those disputes among pedants at the bedside of
a great man whose sickroom is full of strangers. It
is good to get back to the beginnings of our acts,
to the idea which illuminates and justifies them; but
it might be better to consider the suffering body
itself. We must leave the realm of the abstract and
observe the symptoms of our patient with a clinical
eye.

We must come to this. One day the interior dam-
age will be revealed in such a way that many
Frenchmen, now disunited, will forget their dif-
ferences. Then they will share a single passion, a

single desire: that France shall live. "France eternal"; we repeat it as if it concerned a scientific formula or a dogma. It would be much better to face the truth which Péguy perceived on the eve of the other war: "Whole civilizations are dead, absolutely, entirely and totally dead," and which was taken up again by Valéry in 1918: "We civilizations, now we know that we are mortal. . . ." La Palisse is the only philosopher who never deceives himself.

Are we so ill then? To my mind, the worst symptom of the profound disorder which afflicts the French nation is that too often individuals are dragged to disgrace, to dishonor, to condemnation or to a shameful death, not because of the worst in them but because of what is best in them. Consider the officers of Mauberge whose exacerbated sense of injustice drove them to a deplorable act for which they are even now atoning; or that adolescent who believed to be true what his father told him was true, and who enlisted, unhappy boy, in the marching wing of collaboration with the enemy, not as an assassin and a traitor, but as a young being inclined to self-sacrifice. Here, on the one hand, heroes of the Resistance, broken, dishonored; and on the other a boy of eighteen, who is all fervor and purity, is condemned to human degradation— for we know what a prison means at that age: there the angel is delivered to filthy beasts. We know, or rather we do not know, this circle of the social hell: the county jail of Poissy. . . . But that is another question.

We believe that the time has come to consider an internal political policy no longer inspired by the idea of charity or by the idea of justice or vengeance, or by any other abstract notion, but one simply adapted to the exigencies of therapy. We do not doubt that some day all Frenchmen will agree on this point. May God grant that it not be too late.

The Wolf

TRADITIONAL French revolutionaries, even of late, were the offspring of Rousseau. They believed that it was society which corrupts man, that iniquitous institutions and laws ultimately stamp out all the virtues of which we bear the seed in ourselves when we are born. But, after almost two centuries (may poor Jean Jacques rest in peace after having suffered so much), faith in the natural goodness of man has received some rude shocks. What do we talk about every day? I suppose that conversation at the time of the Assyrians, or among Nero's contemporaries, touched on less horrible subjects than ours. Who today would dare deny that ferocity in man exists before all the laws and all the customs? Ascq and Oradour are not acci-

95

dents. "The city was taken and all the inhabitants put to the sword...." As school children, how many times have we not chanted that phrase, which left us neither hot nor cold, and which is the passkey in sacred as well as profane history. It is true that Auschwitz and all the reprisal camps of the Germans, masterpieces of the most heinous techniques, properly belong to one race and one epoch. But a specialist could link them with some sinister tradition without having to go as far back as the Minotaur or the bull of Phalaris.

Yes, man has always been a wolf—a wolf with his own refinements, and who often enjoys befouling those whom he tortures. After nineteen centuries of Christianity we no longer have any reason to believe that we will ever come to the end of this. Man succeeds in disguising himself so well that under the robes of a public prosecutor, for example, he puts on the comedy of justice for honest folk and for himself. Thus a boy of eighteen is sentenced to the putrefaction of the penitentiary because he once gave the Nazi salute. How all those who battened on the Germans during those four years must have laughed: the munition makers, the brothel keepers. They certainly must have quite a laugh when they think of that lad.

It is no longer possible for a thoughtful revolutionary to remain in the tradition of Rousseau. Nevertheless the human wolf, produced by a concatenation of phenomena over which we have no power, must be saved. I imagine that it must be the revolt against all that enslaves and degrades man that keeps our non-Christian comrades from yielding to the temptation of despair in the dungeon of a world with no exit: they are revolutionaries in order not to perish from suffocation.

But we Christians know, we see, what Grace accomplishes every day in some men and women. We are frequent witnesses to the victory of the Angel, and not only among Christians, to be sure! One could even say that goodness is spread very wide, and that it manifests itself even among the harshest if only the wolf within them be asleep. But what a light sleeper he is! All he needs to awaken is to sniff the smell of blood carried to him by the wind, all he needs is to hear the howling of other wolves. And then . . . O my God!

Western Bloc? No: Europe

WORDS often have a malefic power. "West-ern bloc" is a poor expression for an excellent thing. "Bloc" has a hostile ring, it breathes defiance, the distrust of the little vis-à-vis the big. "Bloc" gives an idea of Europe as a trade union of little porters, of disaster victims, or of society folk fallen upon evil days. And in the face of the two mono-liths Russia and America, who envelop us in their immense shadow, "bloc" even has a slightly comic ring about it: one thinks of the rats who banded themselves by their tails to fight the tomcat.... But this does not take into account that now there are two tomcats.

There is no bloc that is not mealymouthed. In our domestic history it was always the label on the worst merchandise. At the time of little Père Combes, an entire abject regime was contained and summarized in this word. But "national bloc" also evokes the helplessness of some, the hypocrisy of others, and a mediocrity which gives an idea of the infinite. Within as without the country, "bloc" has always signified a conglomeration of disparate interests. By definition a bloc is amorphous. How can we avoid quoting old Hugo here?

> *Et dans l'informe bloc des sombres multitudes*
> *La pensée en rêvant sculpte des nations.**

One must be crazy, really, to call "western bloc" that community which bears the old name: Europe ... or to be exact, the prow of Europe, but to which the best of her genius has flowed back. Furthermore, what tactlessness! At the very mention of the word "bloc" all the old mistrust and suspicion awaken to life. Moscow knits its formidable brow. The United States is astonished at this molecular agitation in a negligible corner of the planet.

We must talk to them about Europe. Our great Allies cannot blame Europe for aspiring to turn a

---

* And in the shapeless bloc of somber multitudes
  Dreaming thought carves out nations.

new and unhaggard face to them. It is not in their interests to do business with a needy client, who feels himself to be kept to boot. In us they are looking for an interlocutor, an ally, a friend whose heart overflows with trust and gratitude.

In a recent interview General de Gaulle has defined the political and economic conditions essential for a relative European autonomy. There are also spiritual pre-conditions. Upon reading this master page I seemed to see the heart of Catholicity etched out in the watermark.

There is Catholicity in it, and there is also socialism. Perhaps we shall see them impelled to joint action in Europe, where for so long they have been antagonists. Right now, at any rate, they are the only meeting places with our old enemies. A German Catholic, an Italian socialist, each belongs to the same country, which is also our own. We have a common vocabulary: we can begin to stake out the path; the stream of communication is re-established between us by our first words. It is then that we understand the meaning of our victory: this invisible kingdom, which was the real stake in this war, successfully endured the last of the religious wars, please God. For myself, I shall never forget that the first Germans whom I ran into in my garden, even before my house was occupied, were two young Rhenish soldiers of the Wehrmacht. One accosted me and said in French, "Ah, M. Mauriac, what a misfortune that France has been beaten!" I can still see the bitter, young face under the helmet. They had been punished for attending Mass in the village church on Bastille Day. It was a brief glimmer of light in the shadows of that radiant summer.

I was thinking about this again a few days ago while chatting with an eminent Italian socialist. He also said to me: "Without you . . ." Only this time we exchanged a look laden with hope.

The Eternal Question

NOBODY can predict what an encounter with a dramatic work will awaken in each spectator. But one could say the same thing for most texts of the Bible itself. Everything is in the hands of God, including our works, and He is free to regulate, if I dare say it, their repercussion in each conscience.

We are in a world which is, to be sure, criminal but one that is also penetrated by Grace: the drama necessarily involved in such a conflict arms us in advance, it puts us on guard against everything in and around us which would risk unleashing crime and vanquishing Grace. It seems to me that some Catholics have much to learn from Blaise Couture, the hero of one of my plays: that sinister personage illustrates what remains of a Christian molding of character, once Grace is removed, in a being who has lost faith and charity, in a man who grows rich on what he steals from God. A work which disturbs, perhaps even disconcerts one, should not be condemned just for that. There are such things as healthy disquietude and salutary tribulation. It would be deceit and madness for a writer to let those who read him believe that we live in a reassuring and well-proportioned world.

Clericalism

IF we are to trust the press of the last few days, the *Osservatore Romano* is supposed to have called upon the French to do away with their laic and anticlerical legislation "which has done them so much harm." I greatly distrust these news agencies' dispatches which cite no text—this one above all others since it has all the earmarks of having been lovingly tailored and polished by an expert hand so that *L'Humanité* and *Franc-Tireur* could make the most of it in a flashy front-page display. But even if the *Osservatore Romano* had really expressed this wish, I experience no discomfort of any kind in declaring that it does not even warrant an examination.

And I can't see any reason, if I may take the

liberty of anticipating my critics, for the charge that I am lacking in the respect or the veneration which our spiritual head inspires in us. The *Osservatore Romano* is not for the Catholic what *Pravda* and the *Red Star* are to Communists—not by a long shot, indeed! In politics we are always entirely free not to take its suggestions into account.

The fact is that there is infallibility and infallibility. There is one kind, among certain people whom I know, which is operative in all circumstances, at every instant and in all orders of being, but first and foremost in the political order. It is not the same with Catholics: the Pope is infallible only when he defines a truth of the Faith as the Doctor of all Christians—something which at best happens once or twice in a century.

In the area of speculative argument, a theologian would have little difficulty in extracting all the necessary elements for a condemnation of "secularism" from a certain definition of the word. But that is not at all the question here! In a country populated with Catholics, Protestants, Jews, atheists, rationalists, Marxists—not to mention that last hope of society, the beatniks and their existentialist cohorts —and in which all the confessions, all the negations, all the attitudes of the mind, have their partisans and proselytes, it is quite necessary for the State (unless it be totalitarian) to remain outside the sphere of influence of a doctrine and of a particular cult if it is ever to rise above them all. This is self-evident and warrants no discussion. The neutrality of the State is essential, and it is so to the point where it is useless to speculate about it.

It is a fact that the most disinterested crusades have always ended up by conquering earthly kingdoms. People once believed they were liberating the Holy Sepulcher but actually served the interests of their lords, even gave their lives for the establishment of ephemeral principalities. In the same way the crusaders of our day, in order to liberate enslaved man, often work unwittingly for the construction of an oppressive world. Unwittingly? Is this really true?

Most men are kept alive by engaging in work which transcends them. From the time that the Jesuits more or less resembled the sublime caricature that Pascal etched of them, this must have been the secret of many religious vocations. Today it is the secret of many political vocations: the victories of an order or those of a party console us for our private failures. We shift to them the responsibility of making ourselves masters of the world.

To be a clerical is to divert religion from its objective, it is to make of it an instrument of temporal domination. It is also to make use of the revolutionary faith of peoples in order to gratify the will to power of empires.

The Absent One

IT often happens that midway in his life a man, examining the graph of his destiny, refuses to hold himself responsible before so many public failures and hidden miseries. He incriminates his family, his teachers, the education imposed upon him, the atmosphere of his childhood. He searches for the reasons for his defeat everywhere, except in himself. If his parents are still living, he spares them no reproaches: "You should not have put me in that college. . . . Why did you have to put me in a boarding school?" Or on the contrary: "You should have demanded more of me. . . . You should have been stricter with me. . . ."

We forget these reproaches that we make to our parents, until the day they are no longer there to forgive us for them. Now that they are dead, their poor voices rise in our memory. How poorly they defend themselves! "I thought I was doing the right thing. . . . You were a child who was difficult to understand. . . . Undoubtedly I should have asked advice. . . . I didn't know you were such an unhappy child. . . ."

We can no longer reassure our mother. We shall never again be able to do so. It was necessary for her to die for us to understand what this heart, delivered from life, had maintained in us until the day of its last beat—all in fact that we still preserve of nobility, purity. Undoubtedly at certain turnings in our history it must have beaten faster, used itself up, exhausted itself in order that this force for good in us should not be altogether dominated, destroyed. Even while we were reproaching her, she was—unknown to us—saving us.

Now that she is no longer there, we become conscious of this heritage fled from the center of our inalienable being. As if the poor woman had known that she could depart, that she would take along the tormented youth of her sons with her! As if she knew that they no longer needed either her suffering or her love: the Grace she had merited for them would be enough. When a mother goes to bed in order to die, she seems to confide to her children: "I have done what I could for you. Now it is a matter for God."

But she also leaves us this sorrow of not being able to tell her what we have never said to her. For life only rarely lends itself to these grave words, to these solemn explications in which the aged child can fall at the knees of those from whom he was born. This is why these ceremonies, these honors at the height of life, must have seemed beautiful to us when our mother was still living. These same hands which in other times on the day prizes were awarded placed wreaths on our schoolboy foreheads now can caress, on the inside of our beautiful uniform, these laurels of childhood suddenly grown green again! It seems that on that day and in a single embrace, we would have been able to make her, who put us into the world, understand what human words do not express. Ah! Without a doubt, without ever needing to look for it, the answer to the sublime verses:

> *Lorsque la bûche siffle et chante, si le soir,*
> *Calme, dans le fauteuil je la voyais s'asseoir,*
> *Si, par une nuit bleue et froide de décembre,*

CAIN, WHERE IS YOUR BROTHER?

Je la trouvais tapie en un coin de my chambre,
Grave, et venant du fond de son lit eternel
Couver l'enfant grandi de son oeil maternel,
Que pourrais-je répondre à cette âme pieuse
Voyant tomber des pleurs de sa paupière
                                    Creuse? *

Yes, words or silence, we are sure that we would have found the answer and dried these tears.

I have always preserved a particular gratitude toward the teachers who raised me, for a gesture that they made us perform on the day of our First Communion. Before approaching the Holy Table, we had to leave our seats and go to our parents to ask pardon. But first the priest reminded us that if we had not committed any grave sins and that if we did not feel gravely guilty toward them, we should think about the unknown pains, the future griefs

---

* At eventide
  When the sputtering logs throw sparks in the air,
  Were I to see her sitting calmly in her chair,
  If on a cold blue night of December gloom
  I should see her crouched in a corner of my room,
  Solemn, come from the depths of her couch eternal
  To watch her grown-up child with eye maternal,
  On seeing the tears begin to roll
  Down from her hollowed eyes,
  What would I answer this pious soul?

that they would have later on account of us. At this minute the sensation, if I dare say it, was communicated to us of this eternal gift of God Who sees the falls, the poor risings, the backslidings, the betrayals, the defilements of a whole life in the little boy of ten, with his pure mouth poised to receive the host. But on this day this misery, still latent, was already covered over, forgiven, in the chapel full of sobs where our young mother, who had given up her mourning dress in celebration of the occasion, traced a cross on our forehead.

It is toward this marvelous morning that we go back in our mind, toward which we return across the years, in order to find the certitude that all was known and erased in advance. . . . And undoubtedly, we who possess the Faith, we must believe on so solemn a day, in the invisible presence of the dead who have loved us. But what are our human feasts for those who are in the light? What likelihood that they might descend to the point of this nothingness? Bossuet speaks somewhere of this "great master stroke which will render the saints forever astonished at their own glory."

Against the background of this glory how derisive seems our own! Who can turn their faces away from the Face which they gaze upon? What terrestrial happiness is worth a second's forgetfulness of this joy with which they overflow eternally? Is not this joy of the blessed an impassable ocean between them and us? God Himself prepared this joy, says Bossuet and he writes: "In the depths of the soul He will seek for the place where it will be more capable of felicity." But in the soul of our mothers is not this place the one where our own image is engraved forever?

Here is a thought that consoles us: In the days of her flesh the immense love that a mother had for her children, her worries over health and money, her endless disquietudes, did not prevent her from advancing toward God, against all odds, to find Him and to embrace Him. Why would she not make the same route over again, and why could she not retrace her steps? From the depths of her eternal contemplation, she will be able to find the path of her tenderness again. And perhaps she will not feel herself out of her element there; she will not believe she has changed ambiance. For nothing more resembles the mystery of heaven than this love of woman for the beings she has brought forth.

Resurrection Without End

AN ordeal never turns toward us the face that
we had expected. Something altogether different than we anticipated is demanded of us—something that is at once easier and, though we do not
realize it, more suited to our measure. Our cross is
less heavy than our imagination had envisioned; it
remains nevertheless crushing, though not to the
point where we cannot carry it.

In order to take courage, we ceaselessly repeat
to ourselves, "What a difference in the horror between the present moment and 1940 or 1914!" Undoubtedly. There is no mirage of any kind now,
we believe we see our demands and obligations
clearly, our eyes are no longer distracted or veiled.
They hold out, they will hold out for as long as

will be necessary, with a cold resolution. And they do so without any illusion whatsoever about the world that will appear, once this tide of anxiety has receded.

But there is one truth that we can now dare to look in the face. The City of which we are the workers will never stop being built and being destroyed, even if it will always rise again from the blood and dirt and debris to which men reduce it. It is a work of such infinite sweep and length that it merges with an eternal thought. It will nevertheless always be in peril.

The only work of which we are absolute masters and over which we have sovereign power, the only one that we can dominate, encompass in a glance, and organize, concerns our own heart. A man who dies is a destiny that completes itself, as we say of a poem or a concerto that draws to its close. A given enterprise, measureless and inconceivable to our ephemeral brains, in which generations follow one another and wear themselves out, has no meaning for us except through its repercussions in our private destiny, in this kingdom which is ours, where Grace endlessly lays siege to nature and where nature, sighing, endlessly struggles with herself. Then everything falls in order and takes on a significance, even this very sighing and groaning of the human heart.

I was musing on this while listening to a Suite by Bach this afternoon; and I saw clearly that on the human plane nothing, absolutely nothing, can be brought to perfection here below except the work of art.

Easter: The Challenge to Death

IF the Lord had not risen living from the tomb; if Mary had not recognized Him in the Garden; if He had not manifested Himself at Cephas; if He had not walked at twilight on a road with two disciples as far as the inn where He heard the sweetest words that humanity has ever addressed to Him, "Stay with us, for it is getting towards evening, and the day is now far spent . . ."; if St. Thomas had not placed his fingers in His wounds which no longer bled; if Christ had not manifested Himself to more than five hundred brethren, the majority of whom were still living when Paul wrote his first Epistle to the Corinthians; and if Paul himself had not been dazzled and thrown to the ground at a turn in the road, less by the blinding light than by the unendurable sweetness of this name, "I am Jesus, whom thou art persecuting"—if all this history were not history, we would not this morning be an innumerable throng around the empty tomb wherein our hope reposes.

It is precisely because in our eyes there exists no fact more certain and to which more people have borne witness than the Resurrection, that we find it repugnant to look for only a symbol in it, as do those of little faith, in whose eyes things have never transpired as the witnesses have reported.

Nevertheless there is no trait of this life of Christ that is not reflected in ours, miserable as they may be. From each of her children the Catholic Church requires a resurrection on this holy, radiant day. We are forbidden to be dead persons, we are solemnly enjoined to become living persons again.

I believe they have changed the naïve form of the precept through which we used to mumble our way in former times from our benches in the catechism class. "Thou shalt receive thy Creator humbly at least on Easter." But the commandment remains unchanged. You will receive your Creator despite your crimes, if at least you consent to lay down this unclean burden. Why don't the many creatures grieving over the terrible evidence of hell contemplate this other ineffable evidence: that for as long as they are alive, all power over mercy is given to them. The slightest movement of the heart wrests them from the kind of death which is peculiar to them, and resurrects them from the abyss with which they are all too familiar.

We cannot have our fill of this marvel that each of us is separated from peace and joy only by a sigh. Rimbaud, who believed that he had penetrated so deeply into evil, speaks of this truth, "which perhaps surrounds us with its weeping angels. . . ." It does better than surround the sinner; it harasses him with a monotonous, oceanic fury.

Adolf Hitler

THOUGH he spoke in a Neronic vein of his artistic tastes and of his longing to satisfy them," writes Sir Neville Henderson in his definitive report on the circumstances that determined the end of his mission to Berlin, "I derived the impression that the corporal of the last war was even more anxious to prove what he could do as a conquering generalissimo in the next. . . ."

An artist and an unsatisfied artist, in a word an unsuccessful painter, made Europe pay dearly for his inadequacy. Among the masters of the world the most dreadful belong to this category: a Nero, a Robespierre, carved in the flesh of men a work that might not have been bloody. Poetry is deliverance. We must beware of those whom it has touched with its fire and who, for lack of genius, do not deliver themselves up to it. If Hitler had escaped into a creation, if he had been the renovator of German painting, he would never have prowled around among the weak and small nations of the world, seeking whom he might devour. He would not have treated human nature as he would have treated colors and forms, ideas and dreams, had he been a great artist.

A great artist is not tempted by politics: I distrust those men who envy conquerors. Was Beethoven jealous of Napoleon? Chateaubriand was: a bad sign for *les Natchez*, for *les Martyrs*. Hitler did not have to choose. Incapable of expressing himself according to his first vocation, he dominated men more easily than he was able to deal with political realities and problems.

In the leader the artist is betrayed by two signs, first of all in the very character of his political policy. It tries to carry over the constructions of the mind into the real; and it does not bend to circumstances except under an absolute compulsion. It exerts itself mightily to reproduce a work long meditated, at no matter what cost, the model of which the leader bears within him. The other sign is that the life of an artist who has strayed upon the stage of history puts on quite a show. He lives the drama which he has not written; he himself proposes to the universe the tragic image which he has not been able to fix in a creative work. Only the living matter on which he works does not suffer everything, like clay, like colors, like a white page. In politics, boldness and the contempt for rules cost rivers of blood.

The painter Hitler might have died poor or forsaken like Mozart, or mad like Nietzsche. Sinister deaths, to be sure, but hardly spectacular, and ones from which the world will never make anything but bad movies. As the leader of a party, Chancellor of the Reich and conqueror of defenseless nations, Adolf Hitler could have had only a Shakespearean end—an end of the kind which missed being his at Munich when he already belonged to the theatre and when we listened to him as the protagonist of a tragedy whose characters kill each other for laughs.

Whenever we heard Hitler on the radio, we immediately identified his hideous voice from the very first words—a voice more familiar than that of a friend. It often happens that we hesitate when a voice comes over the air: "Is it Smith or Jones? Do you think it may be So-and-So?" But when it was a question of Hitler, we never confused him with any disciple, we recognized him from the start.

From the reactions of the audience, we always divined that he was addressing not a large anonymous mob, but a body of faithful. What affability in the laughter! What yelpings of tenderness! This was how Robespierre relaxed at the Jacobin Club, this was the same way he accused the wicked, and delivered up his heart. Hitler and Robespierre are the heroes of the works which they could not give to the world. The voice of the *Führer* reached us amplified by the mask of Greek tragedy. He talked fast. He knew that it was necessary to hurry. His demon gave him a dim consciousness of this clockwork hidden above his head, of this spring which was unwinding slowly. His hour had not yet come. It was not yet time for him to leave the stage. His role entailed other replies, other gestures. Millions of men still breathed. Hitler had not yet exhausted his fate.

Did Hitler by chance know the history of Robespierre? Did he remember what followed the arrest of the young girl, Cécile Renault, accused of planning to assassinate the Incorruptible? Thousands of arrests were made at that time in France, as in the *Führer's* Germany. Pitt and Cobourg played the role that later devolved upon the Gestapo. Nevertheless the ninth day of Thermidor was near. No police could have for long defended a being already assassinated in millions of hearts. Hitler, finally, came to that moment of the play—the tyrant no longer dared enter a room in which the police had not first probed the ceiling, the floor, the four walls. The art which he could not put in his paintings ruled his life with a sovereignty surpassing that from which any painter ever suffered. The laws of tragedy remained imprescriptible and the final act had to be bloody.

2

Grace has released man from fate. It conquered the necessity which weighed on the necks of the ancients and made us free—but free also to bend ourselves anew under the yoke. We are free to renounce the freedom of the children of Grace and to insert ourselves once more into the dreadful system in which the ancient world was completely caught.

When the house painter Adolf Hitler signed a pact with fate, he undoubtedly did not measure the power of the corruption of which man is capable. Everything appears to be determined beforehand in such a case, but it remains undecipherable until its consummation. If the tragedy of the *Führer* ever finds its Shakespeare, he will be able to put as an exergue to his play the warning that Jean Cocteau addressed to the spectator of *La Machine Infernale:* "Spectator, behold one of the most perfect machines constructed by the infernal gods, for the mathematical annihilation of a mortal, wound up to the full in such a way that the spring unwinds slowly the whole length of human life."

Undoubtedly Hitler never murdered his father or married his mother like Oedipus. He did not put out his eyes after he saw what he wanted and even dared to see in Munich on that night full of horror. Nevertheless, we judge him as the most wretched among all mortals, more so than Oedipus. For Oedipus became a parricide and committed incest, unwittingly. He himself warned the old men in the sacred grove of Colonus that they should see in him less the author of his deeds than their victim. But when a plane brought Hitler, in the thickest hour of the night, toward his fate, he knew that he was about to murder his companion, his friends, his soldiers, his brothers. Rebels? Yes, perhaps, but rebels who bore no grudge against his life, not even against his authority.... It mattered not, he had to do it, it was his duty, his horrible duty: "Do quickly, what you have to do..." cried out his demon to him.

He was without doubt aware that he would be enjoined to murder twice those who loved him. For murder was not enough; the occult power which held him prisoner exacted of him that he defile for eternity these men for whom he played the part of a teacher, even a god.

It is hideous to dishonor the dead; and if this was ever necessary, what a frightful necessity! But when the one who burdens himself with this task is the murderer himself, still covered all over with their blood, we are gripped by a horror that goes beyond indignation, and no room is left in us for any feeling save pity. How many on the other side of the Rhine must have felt this pity, repeating before Hitler's photograph, perhaps, the words of the Theban people to Oedipus: "Thou who wert a rampart against death for my country, by how many honors did I see thee surrounded on the brilliant throne of Thebes, and now what man, in the cruelest revolution of life, was ever more wretched than you?"

Hitler was free (at least apparently) to spare his victims a third kind of death: spiritual death. Would to God that the thought had occurred to him! But we are very much afraid that he forgot to ask the question Othello put to Desdemona, "Have you prayed tonight, Desdemona?" of those who were about to die by his hand. "Have you prayed tonight, Roehm? Have you prayed tonight, Heines? Have you prayed tonight, you sad and unknown youths whom I myself rescued alive from the Minotaur and whom I now doom to the same agony?"

The special correspondent of the *Telegraf* of Vienna visited the villa where the drama of Munich was enacted. In the dining room he saw a half-filled glass of champagne, a cluster of grapes on a silver platter. . . .

We will never know whether the exterminator fallen from the skies in the midst of this orgy had the final charity to give these souls, surprised in full crime, time to take their spiritual bearings. Like

130

their executioner, these victims had renounced
Grace in order to build their joy beyond good and
evil. Everything is permitted to him who holds
power.... But the man who has chosen to be a
citizen of a world without moral law should never
remove his coat of mail, nor drink any beverage
before a slave has moistened his lips in it, and above
all should believe neither in friendship nor in love,
nor in the brotherhood of arms.

Did Hitler in the last hours of his life believe
that death was not death, that Roehm was still living, that Heines was living, that the young men
who were struck down at the same time were
eternally living? If he believed it, with what dread
he must have met the long twilights of that adorable
summer! For the assassinated have a prime weapon
with which to take revenge on the assassin—memory. What memories must have risen toward Chancellor Hitler, at the same time that the first star
rose in the sky. Combat side by side, defeats and
victories, the acclamation of the crowds around
them, and the fanaticized youth ... "Hitler, we
who loved you!"

And undoubtedly he replied to the phantoms
that pressed on his bed from all sides: "I carried out

a terrible duty; I placed Germany above all, even above my friends. . . ." But the voices from beyond the grave, perhaps, cried out to him the words of Saint-Just: "Nothing resembles virtue like a great crime. . . !" Virtue! Men covered with blood have always stuffed their mouths with this word. It is the mask which Maximilien Robespierre always refastened to his face with a trembling hand. The *Führer* did likewise until the day of his death. But of what use was it to have masked himself and to have sulked like Brutus if, the next time he appeared at an international gathering, he saw all the faces, in an awesome silence, fixing their gaze on his hands?

Philippe Pétain: Halfway
Between Treason and Sacrifice

I

IN my mind there was never any question of making Marshal Pétain directly responsible for the abominations of the Nazis as if he too were to be charged with the horrors of Auschwitz and the rest. In the face of those millions of innocent victims of torture and assassination it was not Pétain who was the hangman. He simply cut the figure of a man who was to be accountable for his own destiny and the particular destiny he gave his country. In a solemn hour, in that interval of time and space when the fate of France hung in suspense, it was Pétain (as a Frenchman, not a Nazi) who deliberately intervened; he assumed a burden heavier (in the eyes of Frenchmen) than any that had ever weighed on human shoulders before. The Marshal was moreover quite aware of what he was doing. He knew that by invoking history he submitted himself in advance to its judgments. "I alone..." he had said.

We know how history responded to Pétain's action. And we have seen how history, justly or not, has judged him. However partisan and impassioned they were, the tribunal, the jurors and the witnesses were only its interpreters. For this "history" to which Pétain appealed does not completely appertain to the future. History in that sense is made, it is woven day by day, and we are all engaged in it. It presses upon us from all sides and we shall not be able to escape it even in death because our memory belongs to history so long as it has not cast us into oblivion.

As for the motives which inspired Marshal Pétain after the debacle, one would have to be very naïve to look for them only in the indictment or in the pleading. The fact that he was an enfeebled octogenarian maneuvered by others, or, according to the public prosecutor, an authoritarian and vain old man, an enemy of the regime and a follower of Maurras, does not exclude the possibility that there may have remained in him some ambition to serve his country once more, to become the ornamental grandfather who would protect the frightened French from the Nazi wolf. The behavior of an old man of his social condition is the result and the sum of his life. Innumerable inherited or acquired tendencies, habits of mind, everything which we understand by professional bent, conspired toward this final and fatal gesture of Pétain's. The more I reflect on it, the more I am loath to make a moral judgment on this sad trial. On the other hand, let his partisans bow, as he for that matter appeared to do himself, before the ultimate consequences of the consent which he gave, in the evening of his life, to the sinister prediction of the political witches from across the Rhine: "Thou shalt be King!"

Many of those who were most excited by Pétain's trial did not seem to have any awareness of its more profound meaning. They seemed to me to lack all feeling for the epoch in which we have been living for a half century, the tragic dimensions of which grow from year to year. I recall a telling remark which Cardinal de Retz once made: "We are going to see things in the next generation alongside which the past two wars with all their horror will seem

like nothing but verdant landscapes and pastorals."
The mass graves only recently opened have barely
been closed again over the pap of tortured bodies.
Hundreds of thousands more still lie under the rubble of great cities. Nations (and not just Russia and
the USA) will soon have the power to annihilate
the planet and the miserable and sublime species
whose members spend the best part of their lives
killing each other on it.

In these shattering realizations of the warnings in
the Apocalypse it is not a small ambition to claim
to lead men. Let him, therefore, who aspires to first
place of any nation first prove himself.

In June 1940 was not Marshal Pétain aware of
the fact that in case of error, France, whom he and
he alone was committing to what he called *his* policy, would have the right to demand an accounting
of him? We do him honor in believing that he
could not escape being conscious of the risk and
that, all the same, he consented to run this risk.
And then the hour arrived for him to pay the price
to the last farthing. But was not Pétain a Christian?
For the Christian, all is Grace. Such must be the
consolation of those who loved the old man. For
those who were faithful to him it could never have

been treason to abandon that tragic old man, who had arrived at the frontiers of life and death, to God, so that they might devote their whole attention to the faceless destiny toward which we are irresistibly moving.

2

I can well imagine that the reactions of my friend Jean Schlumberger, who was an attentive spectator in that dreadful arena of Pétain's trial from the very first day, would be quite different from mine, which are those of a simple man who knows only what he reads in the newspapers. I breathe much less easily than does Schlumberger or any other man in the atmosphere of a tribunal. The appearance of those men who put on a disguise in order to judge their fellows has always aroused an uncomfortable feeling in me, a kind of shame. And I felt such shame with especially piercing sorrow when I read about the judges of Pétain who had the courage to condemn to death an old man to whom they had once consented to link themselves under the Nazi oath.

For us who escaped this atmosphere, the fact remains that the essentials were stated by the prosecution and the defense. The polemics will die out, the arguments of the public prosecutor and those of the lawyers will remain. This thought should comfort those Frenchmen who were irritated, indignant or despairing because of the verdict. For a trial like this one is never closed, the pleading of the case is never finished. At bottom is this not the reason why Pétain wanted to give himself up, why (when he could have escaped this inhuman ordeal) he deliberately chose to submit to it? I imagine that in his eyes the jury which condemned him was nothing but a firing squad whose fury is without significance and counts for nothing. He was appealing his case to other judges on the yonder side of this ephemeral hate.

If Pétain had shamefully sought refuge by some Swiss lake, his case would have been filed away forever. People would no longer have talked about his end without adding the epithet "miserable." But because he gave himself up to our justice, nothing is finished for him. The dialogue of the prosecution and the defense will continue down the centuries. Whatever happens, for his admirers as for his opponents, he will remain a tragic figure, wandering eternally halfway between treason and sacrifice.

I write these things because I believe them to be true, but also for the appeasement of minds. As for those hearts which are so sensitive that nothing will console them, I would first like to remind them of the death sentence imposed on General de Gaulle by a court-martial ordered by Marshal Pétain. According to Maître Payen, the Marshal had said: "It was only a sentence *pro forma:* I never entertained the idea in my mind of carrying it out. . . ." I would like very much to believe that. All the same how lucky that General de Gaulle never fell into the hands of the Vichy ministers alive! He could never have escaped execution or enjoyed the laudable spirit of moderation that Pétain was lucky enough to receive.

3

For the journalist it is both a source of strength and weakness to be far away from the event he discusses. In this peaceful locale where I am staying now, amid meadows refreshed by a recent storm, below snow-capped mountains bathed in an otherworldly light, how can I envisage that overheated hall, bulging with reporters, witnesses, lawyers, and judges, and where only one person seems to be missing: Pétain, that old man who was a stranger to his own destiny, who looks like a statue with a marble countenance, having already entered into a state of eternal indifference.

He listens to the reading of a page of history which concerns him but it has been written forever, and the insults, the accusations, these confused murmurings of love and hate will not change it one iota. This great, impressive and glorious soldier has been promoted to the rank of sinister beings, of the great tragic figures of legend. But at bottom what does it matter to him? He is no longer of this world.

I am too far away from those debates to reconstruct the atmosphere surrounding them. On the other hand, no passion now muddles my conception of the man: I question myself about him, I try to take my bearings, to understand. I don't remember ever having been charmed by him as were most tough-minded politicians. Having been curious to reread what I wrote in my diary at the time of the Armistice following World War I, I could find only two or three polite phrases dedicated to the "Victor of Verdun." And in fact, the first two pages of the *Cahier Noir*, written in July 1940, betray the horror with which I regarded, certainly not the Marshal personally, but the spirit of Vichy, the joyous and moralizing intoxication of those whom the French people had vomited up at every election and who at last had got their revenge—that fatal passion which led them to compromise the most sacred and most holy causes with Nazism.

But today I pose a question which is fundamental for every Christian: Did Marshal Pétain want to betray France? Did he have the intention to betray her? Those Jews handed over to their executioners, those hostages surrendered, those workers deported to Germany, that administration, those magistrates, those policemen become accomplices in things to which a Frenchman cannot even allude without bowing his head in shame, must we consider all that as a lesser evil, as an abomination to which the Vichyite leader thought he must accede in order to avoid a worse one? The accused, it seems to me, would have been wrong to set aside this responsibility, however frightful it may be. From the bottom of the abyss of old age and solitude in which he was three-quarters engulfed, should he have not made this declaration to his judges: "On the day after the French debacle, when the British Empire fought alone against an all-powerful victor, the fate of the world rested on three cards, only one of which was the winning card; but one would have had to be God to turn it up: a German victory—a compromise peace after a long exhausting struggle —an English victory. I wanted to save face in case Hitler triumphed or only half won the war. Since another Frenchman had remained faithful to the English ally, the instinct to save France acted in such a way so that in no contingency would she be completely the loser. But the Frenchman who had gambled on the victory of Germany always knew that if the game was lost, he would become a traitor before his contemporaries and perhaps before history, a criminal guilty of having wanted to link the fate of his country to the destiny of a people at once defeated and dishonored. I took this risk upon myself. An octogenarian, I disgraced myself, I sacrificed my honor in order that, whatever happened, France might be saved."

Thus I force myself to give a too subtle meaning to the conduct of a very old man who in reality was led and used by others. Did he ever understand that Death had forgotten him, that his story was finished twenty-five years ago, that he was the personage of another play, and that he had been pushed into this one by the hands of treason?

4

Whether the armistice Pétain made with Hitler was inevitable or not, it carried within its womb the policy of collaboration with Germany. But to collaborate with the Third Reich whose heinous methods were already known for several years, although less known than they are today, was to lend a hand to crime, to march lockstep with a madman, at once wily and wild; in short, it was to engage France in a political agreement with a monster. The double game here excuses nothing, for there can never be any bargaining without complicity.

But how many people in Europe were also accomplices, more or less? How many are the same today as regards Russia? I am not looking for excuses for the old Marshal; but I believe we must have the courage to see that he did not originate a policy, he was merely the consummation of one. He had had precursors at Munich, and even Munich was not the point of departure: there Europe merely

harvested the fruit of an uninterrupted series of betrayals and acts of cowardice. Before and after that
fatal abdication by the democracies, Hitler never
stopped stockpiling raw materials with which they
furnished him. Up to the very last minute, on the
eve of his greatest outrage, he was benefiting from
the help, overt or covert, of the world.

Marshal Pétain freely assumed responsibilities,
before God and man, from which no one has the
authority to absolve him. But before joining the
chorus of his accusers, we would be hypocrites if
each one of us did not ask ourselves just what each
of us said, wrote, and thought at the time of Munich.
Or what we say in changed circumstances today—
changed and yet essentially the same.

On the day after Munich that great crowd which
acclaimed Daladier when he got out of his plane
(himself surprised not to have to wipe their spittle
from his face) assured the hidden and the open accomplices of the *Führer* that they could go ahead,
and that they would be supported by the weakness
and by the abdication of a whole people. The
French who were in that delirious crowd, or who
shared its feelings, should keep quiet about history's

PHILIPPE PÉTAIN

verdict on Pétain. For is not that verdict their judgment too?

Their trial and also that of nations and parties.
The policy of bargaining with the enemy and of
duplicity, which to our shame the Vichy govern-
ment conducted during four years, was also that
of most of the neutral countries, even when they
were not linked in an open tie with Germany. What
is the use of dwelling on this point, examples of
which abound in the world right now in regard to
Communist Russia and China?

And yet already, doubtlessly, our people were
pulling themselves together, and they said No to
the invader. If we deserved to have Pétain, by the
grace of God we also deserved de Gaulle: the
spirit of surrender and the spirit of resistance are
both incarnate in Frenchmen and they took each
other's measure in a duel to the death. But each of
these two men represented infinitely more than
himself. And since even the least of us shares the
glory of the first man of the French Resistance,
we must not recoil from the thought that part of
us was, perhaps, also the accomplice, the betrayer,
the traitor.

Charles de Gaulle

WHAT we most admire in General de Gaulle is not so much the pledge that he made to France and the world on June 18, 1941. After all, he might not have been able to keep that pledge. But what we are bound to salute, of whatever party we are members, is this: ever since that day he has not ceased to act in accordance with his word. It has guided all his thoughts and acts during more than twenty years. In this lies the quality of his greatness.

We do not believe him to be infallible. Perhaps he will be guilty of the same errors as other leaders before in history. But risks are always present, no matter what side we take.

Even those who were most severe with de Gaulle render a reticent homage to the leader of Free

France. "The experience of power," writes the editor of *Combat*, "has revealed a logic in Charles de Gaulle, an absence of demagogy, which are all too rare in France not to merit our respect and gratitude." This virtue should have been recognized in him at once. But I know why it was not: It is the very absence of demagogy which disconcerts our people. They are not used to their leaders showing them so much respect.

Someone once said to me about the General: "You would think he has no need to be loved. . . ." The fact is, perhaps, that something of a lie enters into the least effort at seduction. A great soul does not seek to please his people, but to serve them. As the Shakespearean hero has said: "I prefer to serve in my manner than to command in theirs. . . ." This is the word of a leader exceedingly indifferent to honors, and very capable of effacing himself, of disappearing. It seems to me that for the moment the French very much desire that General de Gaulle serve them in his manner and we doubt that they will ever have the slightest desire to pour their new wine into old bottles.

148

The Catholic Writer

A S wicked as the world may be, it quickly gives its trust to those who with a certain sense of conviction talk to it about "the only thing necessary." Such matters—which one might think would be matters of indifference to the greatest number in a society which has become pagan—awaken on the contrary both interest and sympathy. It seems impossible to write words which smack of Christianity without unknown persons approaching—as when we shake the oats in the bin and the horses come galloping toward us from the other end of the meadow.

Certain words, we are led to conclude, have preserved their power over starved humanity. It may be that after a half century of effort, the faith of a

people can be destroyed. But hope remains inde-
structible. What writer ever traced the Name which
is above all names and did not benefit from the
tenderness that these two syllables arouse in the
hardest of hearts? "You will be hated by all because of My name"—this is the promise that Jesus
made to His true disciples. It is on this account that
the Christian man of letters, far from drawing on
himself the least hate, appears to the majority of men
who read him in the radiant light of his Master.

If the philosophers of this time, to whom the only
thing that matters is the search for truth and who
claim to delight only in this search, despise Christians who say they have discovered it, this is not
the case with simple and upright people. When we
assert to the latter that truth exists and that there is
a God as well as a Redeemer, they respect in us
their lost faith. They recognize that mysterious
happiness which unfortunately many renounce only
with a sigh.

With what a sorrowful look do hearts full of
disquietude and tribulation observe a man who as-
suringly affirms that, for his part, he has uncovered

the secret of life. Those who believe they no longer have hope have nearly never lost all hope. Without their confessing it to themselves, the Christian represents to them the possibility of healing, of forgiveness, of ennoblement, of eventual rebirth, of a chance to be purified in a world which perhaps is only apparently blind and dumb, a world which they suddenly imagine (what a marvel!) all penetrated, all burning with Grace: a world in which love has become flesh.

For the believing writer, this facility to render the reader attentive and serious constitutes a great peril. Does the idea that one forms of the writer, according to certain moments of his life and particular expressions in his works, correspond to what he is in reality? The world, which judges other men by what is worst about them, often accords the Christian artist the strange favor of seeing in him only the heights. It follows the summit line of this destiny. It is satisfied with these grand affirmations, with these solemn testimonies of a few books and a few articles.

Our constant concern should be ceaselessly to take our bearings, ceaselessly to measure this deviation between the image that our readers form of us and what we really are—at least if we belong to that group of men who have retained a terror of not being sincere. Thereby, the Catholic writer joins again with the great humanist tradition, that of Montaigne. As with Montaigne, it is a question of seeing oneself as clearly as possible, but not in order to delight in oneself. Our aim is to guard ourselves against a formidable peril—the greatest in fact of all perils—for we can unwittingly slide toward what horrifies us most: a writer who does not altogether experience the feelings to which he bears witness in public. Undoubtedly, he is not yet Tartuffe, but he has already made several steps in that direction.

The libertine masquerading under the feathers of an angel makes one shudder. We must dare to look the monster in the face, no matter how far he may appear to be from us. We do not have a role, we do not strike an attitude. We must not write anything which does not express our secret life. But isn't this tantamount to saying we must express what flows, what changes? Then the yellowed words of the most intimate part of ourselves fix and immobilize us in the eyes of the reader, in extreme feelings of joy and fervor. But our soul continues to live, it moves, it no longer resembles altogether, nor at each instant, these reflections of itself which are our writings.

At such moments must it deny them out of a scruple of sincerity? Because it has drifted a little, must it take this deviation into account in order to confess that today it is no longer exactly as it was yesterday? We think, on the contrary, that its exacting sincerity leaves no other way out to this soul except to become again what it is in its highest moments. This sincerity compels it to make an effort, perhaps a heroic one, to return in a sort of empathy to the feelings that its words and writings express. If graces of light are given to us at certain hours of our life, it is not in order that we may exhaust them at one stroke, but in order that we may recall them at moments of tribulation and uncertainty—at the hour, as it were, of darkness.

Let us guard ourselves from giving too much attention to these apparent intermittences of faith, of hope and of love in us. It is a facility for losing caste which some writers give themselves when, under the pretext of sincerity toward themselves, they marry, as it were, their own change and every

CAIN, WHERE IS YOUR BROTHER?

day they destroy the image they formed of themselves the day before.

Perhaps too many men today, haunted by the notion of duration, have lost consciousness of their fundamental "I"—of that part of themselves in which the unity of their being is grounded, despite their undulation and their diversity, and which makes of them an autonomous person, different from all others. Having arrived at this turn in my life, and casting a glance over this long strip of road that cuts across my past, it is always myself that I see there: This child is myself, this adolescent. This young man advances, head bowed, uneasy over the same problems, prey of the same happiness, of the same torment. It is much less my evolution than my fixity which strikes me. Likewise among my comrades.

What most men take for a stream in themselves, for a perpetual flow of states of consciousness, are only eddies around the same confessed or secret, known or unknown, obstacles of themselves. A young writer, Louis Clayeux, has had the patience to search the files of a student magazine for the articles and notes that I published there when I was his age. He had, I believe, an easy time of it to show that the essential character of my work is contained in those stammerings.

Yes, our soul is given to us at the outset; our whole soul, which escapes duration because this immortal soul does not belong to time. What will we do with this depositary? Create its own destiny or passively undergo it? Remain its master or become its slave? The choice depends on our will, according to which we will know how to disentangle in us and set above all the others this instinct of the soul, this unshakable desire for God which will lead us to the living waters through the jungles of gorse and brambles.

To take the side of the soul, to be on the side of truth against one's self, depends on free will. From the moment that a man acquiesces to it, all his fatalities give way, and the conquered passions, stripped of their mask and knife, also collaborate in his spiritual triumph.

How true it is that the truth shall make us free! It is the miracle of miracles: Grace has conquered necessity. In some men it even changes facial features: eyes that were formerly small and troubled open widely and are filled with light; he who had a hideous laugh, suddenly breaks out into a peal of pure and limpid laughter.

Failure? Success? For each one of us the game will be won or lost, according as we have taken sides for or against this soul which will be asked for again from us—according to what we have done with it during this brief passage through a world in which it must be borne, preserved intact, and saved through so many flames!

A pilgrim who knows the goal toward which his love tends, he who knows toward what Jerusalem he is hastening or dragging his feet, in joy or in tears, in peace or in anxiety, the weakest and the most unprovided-for Christian considers himself as a creature ever on the march, until his last breath. On that day—but only on that day—can one say of him that he is a man.